From CLASSROOM to the CLIMB

Lessons of Resilience & Growth

Foreword by Jennifer Branig
Author of The Quickest Way To Write A Book

by Derek Thomas

Table Of Contents

Dedication

To my amazing family. Angela, thank you for your unwavering support and patience through every stage of my journey. Francesca and James, you've been my inspiration and my reason to push forward, even when the path was tough. I know I wasn't always as present as I should have been, but I hope I've shown you that dedication and hard work can build a secure and exciting future. My greatest joy now is being fully present with you, and seeing the bright futures that lie ahead as you create your own lives.

This book is for you, may it remind you always that anything is possible when you're willing to work for it.

With all my love,
Derek

Endorsements

Andrew Lindsay -
Olympic Gold Medalist, Sydney 2000, UW CEO 2010-23

"Derek Thomas has been an inspiring part of the UW story for over 20 years, and it's no surprise to see him putting his journey into words. His passion for helping others grow, his resilience, and his leadership shine through everything he does. This book is another example of Derek leading from the front, and I'm sure it will motivate many more to take that first step to securing a better future."

Duke Al - Former Pupil - Poet & Author of 'Imagine We Trade Bodies With Sheep

As a former pupil of Derek's, now running my own business, I can say he's inspired me both inside and outside the classroom. Having the courage to leave a secure, full-time teaching job to pursue his passion takes a remarkable amount of self-belief and drive, I know, because I've done it myself! I deeply resonate with his informative, motivational wisdom on avoiding burnout, working with purpose, and finding balance between work, hobbies, and most importantly, family life.

If you're looking to make a positive change in your life, this book will uplift you, shift your mindset, and equip you with the tools and strategies to take your own leap.

(His work has been featured by Go.Compare Six Nations Rugby 2025, BBC Wales & TNT Sports)

John Colderley - Former Pupil - Entrepreneur & Ex-Professional Rugby Player

I remember a time in primary school when Mr. Thomas generously offered to coach me during his lunch hour. I wanted to learn the Fosbury Flop and be ready for the county championship. With his support, great athlete and an even greater teacher, we were able to scale new heights together.

(John Secured Investment from Two Dragons on BBC Dragon's Den)

Christopher Lynch - Former Pupil - Author/business owner

Looking back, my time in Mr. Thomas' class feels like it's my own little renaissance; this unexpected time when suddenly science and art and history and maths and storytelling all came together as one. I found my passions for knowledge, curiosity, and creativity in that classroom and most importantly for me, I also learnt that you didn't have to be just one thing.

Back then, I was convinced that Mr. Thomas knew everything about everything and could do anything and he made me believe that I could too.

Honestly? I have yet to encounter any significant evidence to the contrary (at least about him).

Without realising it, I've modelled a lot of my own life and career (or are they careers?) on what I experienced in that classroom. I live in a joyous explosion of doing things I love and somehow getting paid for it. That's what he taught me.

But they do say that every day is a school day. So now, I'm reading Mr. Thomas' book. I'm once again in that classroom that I remember so vividly, ready for my next lesson. I know I will learn something.

(Author of 'Welcome To Neverbury' & 'The Lucy Wilson Mysteries' - From the world of Doctor Who)

Owen Phillips - Derek's PT & Business owner

"I've known Derek for around 12 years, and I can honestly say he's one of the kindest, most genuine people I've ever met. He's supported me through both my professional and personal life without hesitation, always showing up, always listening, and always willing to help. Derek never turns anyone away who needs his time or support. Simply put, he's an all-round great guy."

Stephen Rolley - Former Pupil - Actor/Singer - 'Book Of Mormon' - London West End

I didn't always fit the mould, but school gave me moments of creativity and expression that shaped who I am today, and led me all the way to the West End."

Clare Hingott - Actress/Singer & Entrepreneur

Derek swapped lesson plans for life plans and he's never looked back.

From the Classroom to the Climb is like having a rebellious ex-headteacher yelling from the sidelines, 'Stop putting up with spreadsheets, traffic jams, and beige office walls, there's more to life than this!'

It's sharp, funny, and brutally practical, the push you need to ditch the hamster wheel and start living on your terms.

Robin & Cal Brooks - Entrepreneur, Teacher & Farmer

Derek is an inspiration, Mentor & North to so many! Highly regarded & always gracious & sensitive to people's needs. For Cal & I, Derek is a true friend & the rock companion & professional colleague we all need in life.

Tristan Lee - Health & Wellness Coach

I have had the pleasure of helping Derek to improve his health and wellness for the almost a decade. The goal being to improve his energy, confidence and stamina to achieve his business goals not just for himself but for others too. He has transformed not only his own health but has greatly influenced many fellow entrepreneurs to invest in their own wellbeing too. Well done Derek!

Emma Sullivan - Former V.P. Deutschebank UK & Entrepreneur

Coming from a corporate finance background, I was used to structure and clear targets. Starting my own business felt freeing but also overwhelming, with distractions and moments of feeling stuck. That's where Derek has been incredible. His ability to break things down, tame the squirrel inside and help me take action has been invaluable. He's been my true north, keeping me focused on what really matters.

This book captures that same wisdom and clarity. If you're holding it, you've found a guide who can help you refocus, take action, and build the life you want.

Kerry Ayling - Film Industry

I first reached out to Derek during lockdown while I was writing my first children's book. I'd come from working long hours in the film industry and was busy exploring new paths, but Derek's support gave me the strength to keep going, even when things felt tough.

He's been more than a mentor, he's become a true friend. His advice has helped me shift my mindset and take back control of my time as a busy mum.

If you're about to read his book, you're in for something special. It's full of the same clarity, wisdom, and encouragement he's shared with me and I know it'll inspire you just as much as it has me.

Karen Morgan - Teacher, NGO Worker, Business Owner

I've known Derek for decades, and if there's one thing I can say with certainty, it's that he walks his talk. His proven system for achieving financial freedom is built on real-world experience, clear goals, and unshakable determination. In these pages, Derek reveals not just the "how" but the "why" behind living life entirely on your own terms. Inspiring, practical, and energising, this book is for anyone who knows there must be something better and is ready to go out and get it.

Tom 'Big Al Schreiter, Author, International Speaker & Business Leader

Big steps in life are scary, and we all want security. But when leaving a secure job, and risking the unknown of a business, fear is our biggest enemy. We look for guidance. We look for someone who has gone before us that we can emulate. And that person is Derek. Here are the leadership lessons Derek donates for us to live.

Wes Linden, Author of The Prospecting Game, Host of The Resilience Project podcast & Top Business Mentor

When we face change, fear can make us freeze. We look for people who've been there - who've walked away from certainty to pursue something meaningful. Derek is one of those people. His book gives us the wisdom, honesty, and resilience lessons we all need to keep climbing, even when the path feels uncertain.

Acknowledgements

Our wonderful team - who have been with us on this incredible journey over the last 24 years. Far to many to mention but you know who you are. I appreciate every one of you and consider it a real privilege to have worked with you through the peaks and troughs. You still continue to inspire me every day.

The staff and directors at Utility Warehouse for providing us such a strong vehicle to grow our businesses and chase our dreams.

Charles Davies - For providing me my first opportunity to take charge of a class and encouraging me to pursue my vision of a more experiential learning approach in the classroom

Mark Oakley - Despite some serious mental health challenges you've overcome, you showed me what real work and commitment looks like! Your energy, focus and drive continues to blow me away.

Lloyd Daley for introducing me to my amazing company and showing me there was a better way than the 9 to 5 grind. I will forever be grateful to you.

Steve Rees - for being there at my lowest point. As a former colleague and friend, it's great to see you living the dream!

Huw Jones - Your creativity and love of the arts inspired me so much. We miss you!

Tom Marshall - Your love for adventure and challenge continues to inspire me. Thank you for your support and friendship. Your positivity is infectious!

Team Killi - Gerry, Elaine, Liam, Padraic, Eoin, Darren, Mark, Matthew, Dexter & Taylor. Thank you for making the climb such an enjoyable experience, one which I will never forget, I salute you for the grit and determination you all showed on our journey to the roof top of Africa! Keep climbing!!!

Finally - with gratitude to my mum for her courage, and to Garry, Eddie, Marie, and Michelle, who joined me on the early part of my climb.

Introduction: From the Classroom to the Climb

For many years, I worked in the classroom, giving my time and energy to a profession I cared deeply about. Over time, I began to sense a quiet shift within me. I wasn't sure where it would lead, but I knew I had to explore it.

This book shares the journey that followed.

From the Classroom to the Climb is a collection of real-life experiences, lessons, and reflections that emerged during a time of personal and professional change. It offers an honest look at what it means to step into something unfamiliar, grow through challenges, and discover new possibilities along the way.

Whether you are reflecting on your own path, considering a transition, or looking for fresh perspective, I hope this book offers encouragement and insight for your next step.

The journey continues, one step at a time.

CHAPTER ONE
THE FAST-PACED DECADE

There are moments in life that define us: pivotal points where the path we've travelled for years suddenly diverges. Some changes arrive gradually, like seasons shifting almost imperceptibly. Others strike with the force and clarity of lightning. After twenty-nine years in education, I experienced both.

Standing in front of a classroom, inspiring young minds, and helping children discover their unique strengths wasn't merely my profession; it was my purpose. My approach to teaching was shaped by my own school experiences, which weren't always positive. This drove me to create something better, to lead in a way that made every child feel seen, valued, and capable of greatness.

But passion alone, no matter how genuine, cannot protect us from burnout. As my career progressed from classroom teacher to headteacher, I discovered that leadership, for all its rewards, carries burdens that can slowly crush even the strongest spirits.

The Joy and the Burden of Leadership

The moment I stepped into my first classroom, I felt the electric thrill of finding my calling. Teaching wasn't a job; it was a mission. I witnessed those magical moments when a struggling reader suddenly decoded text, when a shy pupil found their voice, or when a child discovered a talent they never knew they possessed. These moments made every challenge worthwhile.

As I advanced through the ranks (teacher, deputy headteacher, and eventually to my ultimate career goal of headteacher), my responsibilities expanded exponentially. The transition was both exhilarating and overwhelming.

Suddenly, I wasn't just responsible for nurturing young minds; I was managing staff dynamics, wrestling with shrinking budgets, and implementing government policies that often seemed disconnected from educational reality.

Administrative work multiplied, pushing me further from what had drawn me to education in the first place: meaningful interaction with children.

"The function of leadership is to produce more leaders, not more followers." – Ralph Nader

This quote resonated with me deeply as I navigated leadership. I wasn't just leading a school; I was developing the leaders of tomorrow, both on my staff and among our students.

'GROUP LEADER DAY'
NHQ
Wednesday 4th June 2025
1
MILLIO

Fostering Creativity in a Standardised System

One of my greatest challenges as an educator was balancing the requirements of standardised education with my belief in nurturing each child's unique creative potential. The system often rewards conformity, yet I knew that tomorrow's world would demand innovation and original thinking.
I implemented a programme I called "experiential learning" where traditional timetables were suspended for project-based learning. Pupils collaborated across age groups to solve real-world problems: designing playground improvements, opening a travel centre or planning a wedding.

Initially, there was resistance. Some parents worried about "wasted" academic time, and a few staff members felt uncomfortable with the less structured approach. But I remained committed, knowing that these experiences were developing crucial skills no standardised test could measure.

Six months later, something remarkable happened. Not only did creativity flourish, but academic performance improved across core subjects. Students who struggled with traditional learning found their voice through these projects, which in turn boosted their confidence in all areas.

I discovered the power of experiential learning through our Forest School's Writing Project. Some of the children in my class struggled with creative writing because they lacked the real-life experiences that fuel imagination. So, we took them into the woods, toasted marshmallows, played soldier games, and encouraged them to note what they could see, hear, smell, and feel. When they later wrote survival stories, their descriptions were rich and vivid. One boy's work stunned his parents; they couldn't believe he had written it.

It was a clear reminder that when children are given meaningful experiences to draw from, their creativity flourishes and their learning comes to life.

The Importance of Identifying Student Talents

One of education's greatest failings is its narrow definition of success. Some pupils thrive academically, but many others possess talents that traditional education overlooks: music, athletics, entrepreneurship, public speaking, or creativity.

I made it my mission to change this limited perspective.

A defining moment in my leadership came during an INSET training day. I played a clip of **Susan Boyle's** first audition on ***Britain's Got Talent.*** The audience and judges initially dismissed her based on appearance, but the moment she began to sing, jaws dropped in astonishment.

I turned to my staff and said with conviction:

"The crime here is that Susan Boyle went through an entire education system, and no one noticed her talent. Our job is to make sure no child leaves our school without being seen."

That moment sparked a cultural shift in our school. Every Friday, we dedicated assembly time to highlighting pupils' passions and talents beyond academics.

One pupil struggled with traditional subjects but excelled in go-karting. When he stood before the school, sharing his experiences, training regimen, and achievements, his transformation was visible. The pride he carried that day was palpable. As he walked out of that assembly, he was no longer just a struggling student; he was a go-karting expert, respected for his unique abilities.

"A teacher affects eternity; he can never tell where his influence stops." – Henry Adams

Embracing Presence: The Challenge of Family and Career

Whilst I poured my energy into creating an environment where every child felt valued, I was ironically failing to give that same presence to my own family. The demands of leadership had slowly eroded my ability to be fully present at home.

One Saturday morning during breakfast became a turning point in my understanding of this imbalance. As I finally joined my family at the table (after hours of catching up on work emails), my wife turned to our two children and jokingly said:

"Children, this is your father."

Though delivered with humour, her words struck me with the force of truth. I was physically present but mentally absent. My children were growing up with a father who, despite being in the same room, was often mentally back at school: solving problems, planning initiatives, and mentally reviewing budgets.

I laughed at her joke, but inside, I felt the first tremors of recognition that something fundamental needed to change. I was teaching hundreds of children whilst missing the childhood of my own.

The disconnect between my professional mission of seeing each child and my personal failure to truly see my own family grew increasingly stark. I began to realise that the same mindful presence I advocated for in the classroom was exactly what I needed to practise at my own dinner table.

This realisation would ultimately become one of the most important lessons in my journey: The quality of our presence matters more than the quantity of our time. Being fully engaged for thirty minutes holds more value than being physically present but mentally absent for hours.

The Breaking Point: Difficult Decisions

Whilst I remained committed to my educational vision, the financial strain on our school became unbearable: a cruel reality facing many educators today.

One of the most gut-wrenching moments in my career came when I received the annual budget from the local education authority. Sitting alone in my office, staring at those uncompromising numbers, I felt a knot of dread tightening in my stomach. There simply wasn't enough money to maintain our current staffing levels.

I faced an impossible decision: let go of two dedicated teachers or sacrifice my own position.

These weren't just employees on a spreadsheet. These were teachers who had dedicated over a decade to our school. They had shaped hundreds of young lives, just as I had. They had families, mortgages, and dreams that depended on their livelihoods.

I remember sitting across from them, explaining the financial situation. Their faces reflected uncertainty and fear that no dedicated educator should ever have to experience.

At that moment, I knew I couldn't be the reason these excellent teachers lost their positions. I made a decision that many considered reckless: I resigned from my position as headteacher.

I walked away from the career I had built over nearly three decades, but because of the financial safety net I had built, I was able to make this leap even when I had to resign as Headteacher.

It was a scary jump, but I was also very excited to embark on the journey I had envisioned as an entrepreneur 10 years prior to my decision. I am convinced this helped save my life.

It was the hardest professional choice I had ever made.

The Wake-Up Calls

Major life transitions rarely arrive without warning. In retrospect, I can identify several clear signals that change wasn't just necessary; it was inevitable.

The Breakfast Table Revelation

One Saturday morning, as I joined my family for breakfast, my wife turned to our two children and jokingly remarked:

"Children, this is your father."

As I mentioned earlier, though intended as humour, her words struck me with unexpected force. I was physically present but mentally absent, still processing budget concerns, staffing issues, and administrative challenges from the previous week.

I had become so consumed by work that my own family barely recognised me. I laughed reflexively, but an uncomfortable truth had been revealed: my professional dedication was consuming my personal life.

The Forgotten Football Pickup

The wake-up calls continued to intensify.

One evening, during a crucial governors' meeting, my phone rang. My wife's voice carried both concern and accusation:

"Have you picked up James from football?"

My heart plummeted. It was 6 P.M, and I had completely forgotten my eight-year-old son at practice. Whilst I deliberated budget allocations and policy implementations, my child had been waiting, confused and likely hurt by my absence.

That moment shook me. I sat through the remainder of the meeting physically present but mentally elsewhere, imagining my son waiting alone on the sidelines, wondering why his father hadn't come.

My Farewell to School

In the final months before resigning from my headship, I was given the chance to attend a company retreat where I'd been invited to speak. It was on board a five star cruise ship around the Mediterranean. For years, I'd turned down these opportunities because of school commitments, but this time, knowing I was leaving, I decided to go. I took unpaid leave, allowing my deputy to step up and run the school in my absence.

That retreat was a glimpse into the life I was moving towards: one where I could attend events like this, take my family with me, and reclaim the valuable time I had missed with them for so long. It was an incredible experience, spending time with other entrepreneurs who had chosen to change their lives, sharing stories, and connecting with team members also stepping into entrepreneurship.

Yes, I felt guilty leaving school behind while colleagues carried on, but this was a decision I had made a decade earlier. By 50, I vowed I'd leave the stress behind and create a different life. Not everyone approved, teaching is often seen as a lifelong calling, but I knew it was time. I got MAD! I Made A Decision, to change my future.

It wasn't easy. I felt anxious and, at times, afraid. I was abdicating responsibility and stepping into the unknown world of entrepreneurship with no guarantees. But one thing was certain: I was doing this for my family and for myself. And in that moment, I finally understood—this was the beginning of a new chapter, one I had worked so hard to reach.

The Stairs in America

Even as these warning signs accumulated, I continued pushing forward, believing I could somehow regain balance without major change.

Then came another warning, this time from my body itself.

Whilst attending a personal development event in America, seeking clarity about my professional future, I encountered a stark physical limitation. Climbing a simple flight of stairs in the conference centre, I suddenly couldn't breathe. I had to stop mid-staircase, gasping for air, my legs leaden and my heart pounding erratically.

This wasn't normal fatigue. This was my body desperately signalling that something was fundamentally wrong.

The Cardiologist's Verdict

When I returned home, my exhaustion intensified. Focus became impossible. Even simple tasks required extraordinary effort.

Then came the ultimate wake-up call: a visit to the cardiologist that changed everything.

Sitting in the sterile examination room, staring at a scan of my arteries, I heard the words that finally cut through my denial:

"You were very close to a major heart attack."

I needed emergency surgery: six stents to restore blood flow to my heart. Lying on the operating table, a terrifying reality crystallised: had I continued on my previous path, I likely wouldn't have survived to see my children grow up.

Some people never get second chances. I was being offered mine.

The Turning Point

After surgery, clarity emerged through the fog of recovery. I made two fundamental decisions:

1. I would reclaim my health. With the guidance of Tristan Lee (my health and wellbeing coach) and Owen Phillips (my personal trainer), I committed to rebuilding both body and mind.
2. I would take control of my life. No more running on empty, no more sacrificing what mattered most for professional achievement.

At some point, we must all take responsibility for our circumstances. As I reflected during recovery, I realised a fundamental truth: the only person present at every mistake and misstep in my life was me.

We cannot change our past. But we can, with courage and clarity, rewrite our future.

Shifting Focus: What You Pay Attention to Grows

During my recovery and subsequent career transition, I discovered a principle that transformed my perspective: What you focus on expands. Where your focus goes, your energy flows.

I vividly recall attending a company leadership meeting where a new car plan incentive for leaders had been introduced.

Turning to a colleague, I whispered, "What's a BMW X5?" He showed me a picture on his phone, an impressive vehicle, but I couldn't recall ever seeing one on the road.

The remarkable thing happened on my drive home in my Mini. At the first traffic light, an X5 stopped directly in front of me. Continuing along the motorway, I noticed them passing me repeatedly: X5 after X5 after X5.

These vehicles hadn't suddenly materialised; they'd always been there. My brain simply hadn't registered them until they became relevant to my goals. Once my focus shifted, I saw opportunities everywhere that had previously been invisible to me.

This principle applies powerfully to career transitions and personal growth. When we focus on limitations, we see only obstacles. When we focus on possibilities, we discover paths forward we never noticed before.

The Power of Belief: Redefining What's Possible

The difference between stagnation and growth often comes down to a simple question: Do you believe solutions exist for the challenges you face?

I often share the story of **illusionist David Blaine,** who performed a stunt that seemed not just dangerous but suicidal: catching a bullet fired from a rifle in his teeth. Everyone thought he was insane; experts predicted fatal results.

But Blaine approached the seemingly impossible challenge differently. Instead of accepting conventional limitations, he asked: "How can I make this both safe and spectacular?" Through meticulous preparation, specialised equipment, and relentless practice, he accomplished what others deemed impossible.

(Please note: This example is shared purely for illustrative purposes. Under no circumstances should anyone attempt dangerous stunts. The point is about the mindset approach to challenges.)

His team remained anxious throughout the process, convinced disaster was inevitable. Yet Blaine's mindset (focused on possibilities rather than limitations) allowed him to envision a solution beyond conventional thinking.

The lesson is profound: Someone with a fixed mindset would never attempt the "impossible". They'd be paralysed by thoughts of danger and failure. But those who maintain a growth mindset ask different questions: How can this be accomplished? What approaches haven't been tried? Who might help me solve this problem?

This principle guided my transformation from education to entrepreneurship. Rather than seeing my career change as an insurmountable challenge, I approached it as an opportunity to reinvent myself and apply my leadership skills in new contexts.

Key Takeaways

- **Leadership requires sacrifice:** Sometimes, making the right decision means making the hardest decision. True leadership isn't about maintaining power but knowing when to step aside for the greater good.

- **Success without health is failure:** Your body will always warn you when you're overextended. Ignoring these signals can lead to irreversible consequences.

- **Time is the most valuable currency:** No professional achievement justifies missing irreplaceable moments with loved ones. Being present in your personal life matters as much as professional presence.

- **Listening is a superpower:** Whether as a teacher, business leader, or parent, truly listening to others (students, staff, family) can transform lives, including your own.

- **Every wake-up call is an opportunity for change:** The lessons from our most difficult experiences often catalyse our greatest growth. Recognising these lessons and acting on them distinguishes fulfilment from regret.

- **What you focus on expands:** Your attention is a powerful force that shapes your reality. Direct it intentionally toward opportunities rather than obstacles.

- **Belief determines achievement:** The boundaries of what's possible are largely determined by what you believe can be accomplished.

Actionable Steps

1. **Identify your wake-up calls:** Reflect honestly: what signals in your life suggest change is needed? List them and acknowledge what needs to shift.

2. **Prioritise your health before a crisis forces you to:** Choose one aspect of your wellbeing to improve this week: better nutrition, more movement, adequate sleep, or stress management.

3. **Be fully present in your personal life:** Schedule uninterrupted time with loved ones. Eliminate distractions, engage completely, and be emotionally available, not just physically present. I created a 4-block colour code system which is well known in my network. 1. Essential work (Orange) 2. Family commitments (Green) 3. Side-gig (Purple) 4. Wellbeing (Blue).

4. **Make difficult decisions with courage:** If you're holding onto something that no longer serves your values or wellbeing (a position, habit, or belief), develop an exit strategy aligned with your core values.

The path from the classroom to whatever summit you're climbing isn't linear. It involves detours, obstacles, and sometimes starting over. But with each step, properly taken, you build not just resilience but the wisdom to help others navigate their own climbs.

Looking Ahead: The Foundation of Success

In Chapter Two, we'll dive deep into the psychological foundation that makes all meaningful change possible: your mindset. You'll discover:

The Critical Difference Between Fixed and Growth Mindset - Learn how your beliefs about potential and ability fundamentally shape your outcomes. We'll explore Carol Dweck's groundbreaking research and how it applies to career transitions, personal development, and overcoming setbacks.

How Your Thoughts Literally Shape Your Reality - Understand the neuroscience behind thought patterns and how they create biological pathways that either limit or expand your possibilities. I'll share specific techniques I used to rewire negative thought patterns during my own transition.

Practical Frameworks for Reframing Challenges as Opportunities - Master the specific mental shifts that transform obstacles from roadblocks into stepping stones. You'll learn the exact process I used when facing seemingly insurmountable challenges, from health crises to financial uncertainty.

The mindset principles in the next chapter aren't just theoretical concepts; they're the essential foundation upon which all other success strategies must be built. Without addressing these core beliefs first, even the most sophisticated tactics for goal-setting, productivity, or business growth will ultimately falter.

As we explore these concepts together, you'll gain practical tools to identify and transform the limiting beliefs that may be holding you back from your own extraordinary potential. Because the quality of your mindset directly determines the quality of your life, and it's entirely within your power to change.

CHAPTER TWO
MINDSET MATTERS: THE FOUNDATION OF SUCCESS

"*Whether you think you can or you think you can't, you're right.*" – Henry Ford

Identity Crisis

I sat at my desk, going over the budget cuts again. It was clear: we were going to be overstaffed, and two members of staff would have to go. That period felt like setting off an explosion. Anxiety rippled through the staff room. Union meetings were called. Fiery discussions took place. Amalgamation was on the cards. I had to draw up a matrix.

It was no longer "last in, first out": now, it was about your worth to the school.

Fortunately for me, my side gig was generating a decent income. Yes, I'd be taking a massive risk walking away from a headteacher's salary at such a young age. I had always planned to resign at 50. That decision had been made many years earlier.

I recall when I as a boy, standing on the end of the 10-metre diving board, ego bruised, others watching, waiting to see if I'd jump or climb down. And then, someone gave me a little push. Now, sitting at my desk, that was all I needed: one last push.

I had full confidence in the company I'd joined part-time. People often questioned me: How can you leave? What if it fails? But the chairman, Charles Wigoder, who founded the company in 1997, had built something extraordinary. I believed in him and in his dream.

Charles was never going to sell up. He wasn't going to give up his baby for adoption.

What it meant for me was that I'd no longer be working with smaller kids but with bigger kids: adults ready to reclaim their dreams and ambitions. And that excited me.

The decision was made.

I handed in my resignation, and it shocked many. A close friend of mine, another headteacher, asked, "It's not that pig thing, is it?" (Referring to our old logo.) Later, he asked if he could get involved too. I'd been encouraging him for years.

My next thought was: How will they manage without me?

Ironically, a few years later, I found out. They simply replaced my cog with another cog. And when I was seriously ill, recovering from heart surgery, I realised something: no cards from the school, no messages, no calls. Except one, Maggie, who previously worked as a nurse.

The rest were drowning in their own workloads.

Now, for the first time in a long time, I was excited about the future. It felt like a massive pressure had lifted from my shoulders.

Like summiting Kilimanjaro, I could finally breathe again.

I'd reached the summit of my school career, and the vision for my future looked amazing.

The Mindset Revolution

There was a time in my life when I let doubt control my decisions. I played it safe, avoided risks, and stayed in my comfort zone because it felt secure. But the problem with comfort zones is that they don't help us grow.

Over the years, I learned that success isn't about talent, luck, or intelligence. It's about mindset. The way we think determines the way we live.

The difference between those who succeed and those who stay stuck isn't their skills; it's their ability to push past fear, embrace challenges, and keep going despite failure.

This chapter is about how you can reprogram your mind for success: how to stop letting fear, doubt, and self-limiting beliefs hold you back.

The moment I submitted my resignation letter, something profound shifted in my thinking. For years, I had defined myself by my role as an educator. I was "Derek the headteacher", "Derek the leader", and "Derek who solves problems". But who was I when I stripped away those titles?

This identity crisis became the catalyst for one of the most important discoveries of my life: our thoughts create our reality, and we have far more control over them than we realise.

Mindset: The Foundation of Success

Success doesn't start with actions; it starts with thoughts. The way we think about ourselves, our abilities, and our circumstances shapes our entire reality. Your mindset acts as the operating system of your life, guiding the choices you make, the risks you take, and the opportunities you recognise.

During my transition from education to entrepreneurship, I discovered the profound truth behind Dr Carol Dweck's research on mindset. There are two primary types of mindsets that influence our outcomes:

Fixed Mindset: People with a fixed mindset believe that their intelligence, abilities, and talents are static. They see failure as proof of their limitations rather than as an opportunity for growth. They avoid challenges, fearing they might expose their weaknesses.

Growth Mindset: People with a growth mindset believe that abilities can be developed through dedication and hard work. They see challenges as opportunities to grow and failure as a stepping stone to success. They seek feedback, embrace effort, and persist in the face of obstacles.

The key to success is shifting from a fixed mindset to a growth mindset. This shift doesn't happen overnight, but with conscious effort, anyone can cultivate a mindset that fosters resilience, learning, and achievement.

When I first learned about network marketing, my fixed mindset kicked in immediately. "I'm not a salesperson," I told myself. "I don't have the right personality for this." These thoughts were limiting beliefs disguised as facts.

But as I began to study successful people in the industry, I noticed they weren't necessarily the most charismatic or naturally gifted. They were the ones who believed they could learn, grow, and improve. They had adopted a growth mindset that allowed them to see every conversation as a learning opportunity, every "no" as a step closer to a "yes".

The Neuroscience of Change

Understanding how our brains work is crucial to changing our mindset. Neuroscience has shown us that our brains are remarkably adaptable throughout our lives, a quality called neuroplasticity. This means we can literally rewire our thinking patterns.

When I was struggling with the decision to leave education, my brain was running old programmes: "You need security," "You can't start over at your age," "What will people think?" These thought patterns had been reinforced over decades of conditioning.

But I learned that every time we think a new thought or take a new action, we create new neural pathways. The more we repeat these new patterns, the stronger they become, whilst the old pathways gradually weaken.

This scientific understanding gave me hope. It meant that the limiting beliefs I'd carried for years weren't permanent fixtures; they were changeable programmes that I could update.

Reframing Failure and Overcoming Resistance

One of the biggest mindset shifts involves redefining failure. Instead of seeing it as something to avoid, successful individuals view failure as feedback. Every setback carries valuable lessons that help refine strategies and improve decision-making.

A personal example of this was when I decided to implement a new training regime. Initially, my brain resisted the change. My routine had been deeply ingrained: work, calls, appointments, and daily habits that didn't include structured exercise. Suddenly, incorporating physical training disrupted that pattern, and my brain reacted with resistance.

At times, I struggled to stay consistent, but I turned to two books that transformed my approach: The Consistency Chain and

Atomic Habits. They reinforced a crucial principle: if I wanted different results, I had to change my approach. My old routine had been automated by my brain, but by repeatedly engaging in my new habit, I began rewiring those pathways.

I often say, "If you keep doing what you've always done, you'll keep getting what you've always got." Change requires intentional effort. It's uncomfortable at first, but as I continued pushing through, my brain adapted, and soon, training became a natural part of my day.

The resistance I felt wasn't a sign that I was on the wrong path; it was simply my brain's way of trying to keep me in familiar territory. Once I understood this, I could push through the discomfort with confidence.

How Our Brains Keep Us Stuck

Our brains are wired for survival, not success.

Thousands of years ago, avoiding danger meant staying alive. Our ancestors knew that taking risks (exploring unknown territory, eating unfamiliar food, confronting predators) could mean death.

That's why our brains are programmed to avoid discomfort, uncertainty, and change.

The problem? That same survival instinct now holds us back.

Public speaking feels terrifying because our brain still sees a crowd as a potential threat.

Starting a business feels risky because our brain prefers security over potential failure.

Changing careers feels overwhelming because our brain loves familiarity.

The truth is, your comfort zone is not a place of safety; it's a prison.

If we only do what feels "safe", we never grow.

Understanding this biological reality was liberating for me. When I felt fear about leaving my secure position, I could recognise it as an ancient survival mechanism rather than an accurate assessment of actual danger. This awareness allowed me to act despite the fear.

The Power of Focus and Thought Filtering

Our brains process an estimated 70,000 thoughts per day, filtering out what's considered "unimportant" so we can focus on what truly matters. But this filtering system can work against us if we don't take control of our thoughts.

For example, I recall being in the staff room as a teacher. A colleague would come in and say, "I've had an awful morning: my Year Six class was terrible." Another would join in, adding their bad experience. Soon, everyone focused on negativity, reinforcing a bad day before heading back to teach.

Our minds latch onto what we focus on, and if we focus on negativity, we'll find more of it. But if we intentionally look for positives (even in difficult situations), we shift our experience. I made it a habit to catch pupils doing something good rather than only addressing their mistakes. That simple shift changed classroom dynamics and pupil behaviour.

The same principle applies to our personal and professional lives. If we train ourselves to focus on progress, solutions, and opportunities rather than limitations, our minds will begin filtering in more of what we want rather than what we fear.

This filtering system explains why, after learning about the BMW X5 incentive in my business, I suddenly started noticing these cars everywhere. They had always been there, but my brain hadn't deemed them worth noticing until they became relevant to my goals.

Rebuilding Identity After Major Change

One of the most challenging aspects of leaving education was rebuilding my identity. For nearly three decades, I had been defined by my role in schools. When people asked what I did, I had a clear, socially respected answer: "I'm a headteacher."

Suddenly, that identity was gone. Who was I now?

This identity crisis is common during major life transitions. We become so attached to our roles that we forget these are simply labels, not our true essence. The real work of transformation involves discovering who we are beneath these external identities.

I had to learn to separate my worth from my role. My value as a person wasn't diminished because I was no longer a headteacher. My skills, experience, and character remained intact; I was simply applying them in a new context.

This process required conscious effort. I had to catch myself when I introduced myself using past tense: "I used to be a headteacher." Instead, I learned to focus on my current identity: "I help people achieve their goals and build better lives."

Language shapes reality. By changing how I spoke about myself, I gradually shifted how I thought about myself.

The Stories We Tell Ourselves

Every day, we tell ourselves stories about who we are, what we're capable of, and what's possible for our future. These internal narratives become self-fulfilling prophecies.

For years, I told myself stories that seemed factual but were actually limiting beliefs:

"I'm not good at languages"

"I'm too old to learn new tricks."

"I'm not a natural salesperson."

"I need the security of a regular salary."

Each of these stories felt true because I had evidence to support them. But evidence can be selective. We tend to notice information that confirms our existing beliefs whilst ignoring contradictory evidence.

When I decided to challenge these stories, I discovered that many of them were simply outdated programmes running in my subconscious. The "evidence" I had been collecting was biased towards confirming what I already believed.

Changing these stories required conscious effort. I had to actively look for evidence that contradicted my limiting beliefs. I sought out examples of people who had made similar transitions successfully. I celebrated small wins that proved my new capabilities.

Gradually, the old stories lost their grip, and new, more empowering narratives took their place.

Lessons from My Journey: Overcoming Fear

Fear is one of the biggest roadblocks to success. I've faced it in multiple areas of my life: public speaking, business decisions, and even physical challenges. But through these experiences, I learned that fear loses its grip when we act despite it.

Lesson 1: Facing the Fear of Public Speaking

I remember the first time I had to speak in front of a large audience. My heart raced, my palms sweated, and my mind tried to convince me to back out. But instead of giving in to the fear, I reminded myself why I was doing it: to inspire, to share my knowledge, and to grow.

The breakthrough came when I realised that my fear wasn't about the audience; it was about my internal dialogue. I was terrified of being judged, of making mistakes, of not being good enough. But when I shifted my focus from my own insecurities to the value I could provide to the audience, the fear diminished. Confidence doesn't come from waiting until you feel ready; it comes from taking action despite fear.

Lesson 2: Embracing Uncertainty in Business

When I first started my business, doubts flooded my mind. What if I fail? What if no one believes in me? But I realised that every successful entrepreneur once stood at the edge of uncertainty, just like I did. So, instead of fearing failure, I chose to embrace it as part of the journey.

I learned to reframe uncertainty as excitement. Both emotions create similar physical sensations: increased heart rate, heightened alertness, nervous energy. The difference is in how we interpret these sensations. By consciously choosing to see uncertainty as anticipation rather than anxiety, I transformed my experience.

Lesson 3: Pushing Past Physical and Mental Limits

Climbing Mount Kilimanjaro was one of the toughest physical and mental challenges I have ever faced. Negative thoughts tried to hold me back: people warned me about the dangers, questioned if I was too old, and my own brain fed me doubts. But I had prepared. I trained on a step machine daily, knowing that consistency would build my endurance.

When doubt crept in during the climb, I told myself: Just take one more step. That mantra carried me to the summit, proving that our limitations are often illusions created by our minds.

The mountain taught me that success isn't about avoiding discomfort; it's about pushing through it. Every step towards the summit was a step away from my comfort zone, but it was also a step towards proving to myself what was possible.

The Role of Environment in Mindset

Our environment significantly influences our mindset. The people we spend time with, the media we consume, and the physical spaces we inhabit all shape our thinking patterns.

When I was struggling with the decision to leave education, I realised that most of my social circle consisted of other educators who shared similar limiting beliefs about security, risk, and career changes. Their well-meaning advice was actually reinforcing my fears rather than encouraging my growth.

I made a conscious decision to expand my environment. I started attending business-development events, reading books by entrepreneurs, and listening to podcasts about personal growth. I sought out mentors who had made similar transitions successfully.

This new environment gradually shifted my thinking. Instead of being surrounded by reasons why I couldn't succeed, I was immersed in examples of people who had overcome similar challenges.

Practical Strategies for Mindset Transformation

Changing your mindset requires consistent practice. Here are the strategies that proved most effective in my own transformation:

1 Morning Mind Programming

I developed a morning routine that set my mental state for the day. This included reading empowering content, listening to educational podcasts, and reviewing my goals. Starting each day with positive, growth-oriented input helped programme my mind for success.

2 Thought Auditing

I began paying attention to my internal dialogue throughout the day. When I caught myself thinking limiting thoughts, I would consciously challenge them. "Is this thought helpful? Is it true? What evidence contradicts this belief?"

3 Surrounding Myself with Growth-Minded People

I intentionally sought out relationships with people who were pursuing their own growth and challenging their limitations. Their energy and perspective became contagious.

4 Celebrating Small Wins

I learned to acknowledge and celebrate progress, no matter how small. This helped rewire my brain to focus on advancement rather than perfection.

5 Reframing Challenges as Opportunities

Instead of seeing obstacles as problems, I trained myself to ask, "What can I learn from this? How might this challenge help me grow?"

The Compound Effect of Mindset

The changes in my thinking didn't happen overnight, but they compounded over time. Each small shift in perspective built upon the previous ones, creating momentum that eventually led to dramatic transformation.

Six months after leaving education, I barely recognised my old thinking patterns. The fears that had once seemed insurmountable now appeared manageable. The goals that had once seemed impossible now felt achievable.

This transformation wasn't the result of one dramatic moment; it was the accumulation of thousands of small mental shifts, practised consistently over time.

Key Takeaways

* Your brain tries to keep you safe, but real success lies outside your comfort zone.
* Fear is normal, but action is what separates success from regret.
* Your mind filters what you focus on: train it to see opportunities, not limitations.
* Consistency rewires your brain: small, repeated actions create big changes.
* Your thoughts shape your reality: what you think, you become.
* Identity is flexible: you are not your role or your past circumstances.
* Environment influences mindset: choose your influences consciously.
* Mindset change compounds over time: small shifts lead to dramatic transformation.

Actionable Steps

1. **Identify your limiting beliefs:** Write down five beliefs you hold about yourself or your capabilities that might be holding you back. Question each one: Is this absolutely true? What evidence contradicts this belief?

2. **Audit your environment:** Evaluate the people, media, and information you're regularly exposed to. Are they supporting a growth mindset or reinforcing limitations? Make changes where necessary.

3. **Practise thought challenging:** For one week, catch yourself whenever you think a limiting thought. Immediately challenge it and replace it with a more empowering alternative.

4. **Create a morning routine:** Develop a 15-minute morning practice that programmes your mind for growth. This could include reading, journalling, meditation, or goal review.

5. **Seek evidence of possibility:** Find three examples of people who have achieved something you currently believe is impossible for you. Study their journey and identify transferable strategies.

6. **Reframe one fear:** Choose one fear that's been holding you back. Practise reframing it as excitement about growth and possibility. Take one small action despite the fear.

7. **Start a success journal:** Each evening, write down three wins from your day, no matter how small. This trains your brain to focus on progress and possibility.

Remember: Your mindset is not fixed. With conscious effort and consistent practice, you can reprogram your thinking patterns to support the life you want to create. The same brain that has been protecting you with limiting beliefs can be trained to empower you with unlimited possibilities.

The foundation has been laid. Now we're ready to build upon it with goals that truly stick.

Looking Ahead: The Foundation of Success

In Chapter Three, we'll explore the crucial next step in your transformation journey: creating goals that actually work. You'll discover:

Why Most People Fail at Goal-Setting – Learn the common mistakes that doom 92% of goals to failure before they even begin. I'll share the specific errors I made in my early attempts at change and how recognising these patterns transformed my approach.

The Power of Clarity and Writing Down Your Vision – Understand why written goals are 42% more likely to be achieved and discover the exact process I use to create crystal-clear objectives that your brain can't ignore.

SMART Goals vs. Emotional Goals: What Works Best – Explore the limitations of traditional SMART goal frameworks and learn about emotional goal-setting that connects to your deepest motivations and values.

How My Goals Evolved from Survival to Purpose – Follow my personal journey from setting goals based on fear and scarcity to creating objectives rooted in purpose and contribution. This shift changed everything about how I approached challenges.

The "Why + How + When" Formula – Master the specific framework that transforms vague wishes into concrete action plans. You'll learn how to connect your goals to compelling reasons, clear strategies, and specific timelines.

The goal-setting principles in the next chapter aren't just about achieving more; they're about aligning your actions with your values and creating a life of genuine fulfilment. Without clear, emotionally compelling goals, even the strongest mindset will lack direction and focus.

As we explore these concepts together, you'll gain the tools to set goals that pull you forward rather than push you into action, goals that energise rather than exhaust you, and goals that create lasting change rather than temporary motivation.

CHAPTER THREE
SETTING GOALS THAT STICK

It's a startling fact that only 3% of people ever set goals. This means that a staggering 97% go through life without a clear understanding of what they want, when they expect to achieve it, and how to get there. If you're reading this book, you've already taken a crucial step toward joining that 3% who deliberately design their future rather than simply letting life happen to them.

From a young age, I knew I wanted success. My goal was to become a teacher and improve upon the educational experiences I had during my own schooling. However, at that time, I lacked the necessary academic qualifications needed to embark on this journey. This underlines the critical importance of making a well-structured plan.

"A goal without a plan is just a wish."
– Antoine de Saint-Exupéry

Potpourri Pots: A Childhood Story

My mother was doing everything she could to generate an income and feed her five children. I was deeply involved in athletics at the time, something I was good at, and something I could lose myself in completely. But what I needed, and what my mother simply couldn't afford, was kit: shoes, running vests, training gear.

Then came an opportunity. My brother and I were offered some flexible work with a man known as John the Potter. He had a stall at the market where my mum also worked. Our job was to help him fill the handmade pottery pots he sold with dried flowers that had been scented with oils.

I didn't enjoy the work at all. It was monotonous. But my drive wasn't about enjoyment; it was about earning enough money to buy what my mum couldn't: running kit and trainers.

We set up a system. A box of dried flowers. Glass jars of scented oils. The job involved rubbing the oils into the flowers and filling the oval pots. It was repetitive but flexible; we worked evenings, weekends, and school holidays.

What I did enjoy were the results. I could finally afford the tidy running vests, the shorts, and the trainers I needed to compete with the local athletics club.

In a strange way, it's not so different from the company I work with now. We offer everyday things: nothing flashy. Energy, broadband, mobile. Essential, not exciting. But by encouraging people to use those services, we create massive benefits for ourselves and for others. It helps reduce their costs and generates real income for those willing to put in the effort.

Back then, the oils would soak into our skin, and the smell was tough to wash out, especially when we worked late and didn't even shower! We'd walk into school stinking of lavender or rose or god knows what and became the laughingstock. But if there was one upside, it was that we brought some genuinely nice smells into those sweaty teenage classrooms.

Of course, the teasing led to fights. And the fights led to trouble with teachers and authority. But that was just part of life. Kids are cruel. If it hadn't been the flower scents, they'd have picked on something else.

What matters is what the experience taught me.

It built discipline. It sparked self-reliance. And it planted the seeds of something bigger: my early entrepreneurial spirit.

This childhood experience of working toward a specific goal (affording proper athletic kit) taught me something fundamental about goal-setting that I've carried with me ever since. The goal itself mattered less than what achieving it required of me: discipline, persistence, and the willingness to endure temporary discomfort for long-term gain.

The Mountain Ahead

It could have been easy for me to give up on my educational aspirations entirely, much like how many people enthusiastically join gyms in January with the intention of getting fit but abandon their resolutions by February as reality sets in. People frequently set ambitious challenges but ultimately fail because our brains are not inherently designed for sustained action toward long-term goals.

My early experiences in education were challenging. Being sent to a special school for behavioural difficulties could have been the end of my educational aspirations. But instead of accepting this as my destiny, I began to set small, incremental goals. First, to control my behaviour enough to return to mainstream education. Then, to pass maths exams with the help of Mr. Edwards and my art history A-level exam with

Mr. Coard. Each goal built upon the previous one, eventually leading to teacher training.

One particularly enormous goal for me was becoming a teacher and eventually running my own school: a challenge that often felt overwhelmingly daunting. Looking at a challenge as a mountain can intimidate you into inaction; it's too tall, too high, too difficult. But if you view it as a staircase going up that mountain (one small step at a time) you're far more likely to begin your ascent.

This principle proved crucial when I faced the seemingly impossible transition from troubled pupil to educational leader. Each qualification I earned, each positive report I received, each small success in the classroom, was a step on that staircase. Without breaking down the mountain into manageable steps, I would have been paralysed by the enormity of the transformation required.

The Power of Small Steps

Setting effective goals requires establishing stepping stones toward those larger objectives whilst adopting the mindset that if you truly desire something significant in your life, you must create an actionable plan.

In June 2024, as part of a big fitness goal, I took on the challenge of climbing Kilimanjaro: the world's largest free-standing volcano standing nearly 20,000 feet above sea level. During one particularly gruelling night climb after an entire day's trek through rugged terrain, we found ourselves just two hours away from reaching the summit around 6:30 AM when fatigue hit us hard.

As I looked up towards what seemed like an unreachable peak adorned with tiny head torches zigzagging upwards into the vast expanse above me, feelings of despair began creeping in. I seriously contemplated giving up. I sat down, thinking about how I would explain my failure to everyone back home who knew about this challenge. This felt eerily reminiscent of moments in my professional life when a goal seemed too distant, too difficult.

But instead of surrendering, I focused intently on taking just one more step forward whilst tracking another climber ahead who appeared fitter yet equally determined. I reminded myself of the goal-setting principles I teach others: focus on the next step, not the entire mountain.

"*The man who moves a mountain begins by carrying away small stones.*" – Confucius

Miraculously, two hours later at precisely 6:24 AM, I summited Kilimanjaro! The breathtaking view from Uhuru Peak re-energised us as dawn broke over its majestic landscape. It became abundantly clear how vital perseverance is in achieving one's goals against all odds.

This same approach helped me navigate the path from troubled pupil to classroom teacher to headteacher. Each promotion, each new responsibility, was a step up that mountain. When I became deputy head, the prospect of ultimate leadership responsibility sometimes felt as daunting as that pre-dawn climb on Kilimanjaro. But by focusing on mastering one skill at a time, one challenge at a time, I eventually reached that summit as well.

This is the essence of effective goal-setting: breaking down seemingly impossible mountains into manageable steps whilst keeping your focus on the immediate next action rather than becoming overwhelmed by the entirety of the journey.

The Emotional Connection

Reflecting on transformative journeys reminds us why we pursue aspirations in the first place: How will achieving them affect us emotionally? A mentor once advised me about setting clear objectives based not merely on fleeting desires but rather grounded intentions. What do we genuinely wish for deep down?

During stressful times throughout my school years, someone suggested writing down my goals would help clarify where exactly I was headed, and indeed it worked wonders! Thus began my practice: diligently jotting down everything from desired experiences (like visiting certain places) alongside personal growth ambitions.

The emotional connection to my teaching goals was particularly strong. Having experienced the pain of being misunderstood and undervalued as a child in the education system, I was driven by a deep desire to create a different experience for other children. I wanted to build schools where every child felt seen and valued, where talents were recognised beyond academic achievement. This emotional driver was critical when obstacles arose; it provided the "why" that kept me going when the "how" seemed impossible.

The same emotional connection sustained me through my health transformation after my heart surgery. It wasn't just about becoming fitter; it was about being present for my children's future, about modelling resilience, about proving that setbacks don't define our limits. When the physical challenges of rehabilitation felt overwhelming, this deeper purpose pulled me forward.

Stephen's Story: Discovering Hidden Talents

As educators, we have a unique opportunity to help pupils discover their own hidden talents and strengths. Let me share Stephen's story with you.

When Stephen was a young pupil at my school, he was constantly coming up against authority. He couldn't sit still for very long, and it wasn't unusual for him to be sent to me after a clash with one of his teachers. Over time, I began to realise something important: Stephen wasn't defiant for the sake of it; he simply wasn't built to sit behind a desk for hours. He was a mover, a kinaesthetic learner, someone who needed to be active to thrive.

A clue came to me outside of school, at my local gym. I happened to notice a board listing past tennis champions, and there, under 2008, was Stephen's name. He had won the junior tennis championships. It confirmed what I was starting to understand: Stephen's energy and drive weren't problems to be fixed; they were strengths to be nurtured.

Shortly before the first lockdown, I had a chance to catch up with him. He told me, almost casually, that he had landed a cover lead role in The Book of Mormon in the West End. I was blown away. In that moment, it all made sense: Stephen was a performer. Whether on the tennis court, in the classroom (sometimes for the wrong reasons), or on the stage, Stephen was at his best when he was allowed to move, to express himself, to connect with others.

Stephen had an uncanny ability even as a child: he could predict within two seconds how a supply teacher's day was going to go. Looking back, it reminds me just how often we try to push young people through a curriculum that doesn't always serve their natural talents and instincts, rather than harnessing the incredible gifts they already have.

More recently, Stephen invited me to see him perform. I took a few friends, and we sat right in the front row. I'll never forget it: halfway through the show, one of my friends whispered, "I think he winked at me!" I smiled and said, "No, he's just recognised his old headteacher."

It was a wonderful, emotional moment: to see Stephen in his element, doing what he loved, and thriving. He had found a way to turn his passion into his career. He was not just performing; he was earning a living doing what made him feel most alive. Watching him on that stage, I felt so proud and quietly hopeful that more young people like Stephen would be seen for who they truly are.

Stephen's story illustrates something crucial about goal-setting: the most powerful goals align with our natural talents and authentic selves. When we set goals that honour who we really are, rather than who we think we should be, we tap into a source of energy and motivation that makes achievement feel inevitable rather than forced.

E BOOK OF MORM
9 TONY AWARDS
BEST MUSICAL
PRINCE OF WALES
A MASSIVE
HIT
BLAST
HIT

The Brain Dump Method

The process I recommend follows these steps:

Brain Dump: Write down 100 things you want to do, see, have, or become in your lifetime.

Categorise: Sort your aspirations into timeframes: 1-year goals, 3-year goals, 5-year goals, and 10-year goals.

Prioritise: Select your top four from each timeframe.

Connect Emotionally: For each goal, write down WHY it matters to you. What emotions will achieving it bring?

Narrowing extensive lists into manageable stepping stones categorised by yearly milestones transforms vague dreams into actionable plans.

This method worked powerfully for me during my career transition. When I first did this exercise, I was surprised by what emerged. Many of my goals weren't about career advancement or financial success; they were about experiences, relationships, and personal growth. This insight helped me recognise that my unhappiness in education wasn't just about the job itself but about how it was preventing me from pursuing these deeper aspirations.

Visualisation: Making Goals Tangible

Visualisation played an essential role too; creating vision boards provided tangible reminders each day whilst working tirelessly towards those aspirations kept motivation alive amidst busy teaching schedules!

For instance, one of my short-term goals involved attending Manchester City games with my son, which fostered cherished memories together despite initial financial constraints. The emotional connection I felt (not having spent much time with my own father) made this goal particularly meaningful. It wasn't just about watching football; it was about creating a bond with my son that I never had with my father.

MANCHESTER CITY F.C.
MANCHESTER CITY

During my headteacher days, I kept a small photo in my desk drawer of the kind of school I wanted to create: happy children engaged in diverse activities, not just academic work. On particularly challenging days dealing with budgets, staff issues, or administrative burdens, I would take a moment to look at that image and reconnect with my purpose.

Longer-term dreams included swimming with dolphins in Orlando with my daughter alongside assuming leadership roles within education over ten years' time, all achieved through consistent effort fuelled by emotional connections deeply intertwined into each objective.

> "*The trouble with not having a goal is that you can spend your life running up and down the field and never score.*" – Bill Copeland

The Salmon Effect: Purpose Behind Goals

Yet many struggle because they lack both direction and purpose behind their ambitions. The story of salmon illustrates this beautifully! Salmon spawn upstream far away from their ocean home, ensuring survival against predators until adulthood returns them homeward bound despite arduous battles faced navigating rocky waters along treacherous paths.

Like the salmon, we need a compelling purpose driving our goals. Without this purpose (this "why") we're likely to give up when obstacles arise.

This resonated strongly with me during my transition from education to entrepreneurship. Leaving behind the security of a career I'd built over 29 years was terrifying. What sustained me through this change was connecting to my deeper purpose: helping people transform their lives through better understanding of mindset, goals, and leadership principles. This compelling "why" pulled me forward even when the path seemed uncertain.

Maintaining Momentum

Effort matters tremendously in goal achievement, as demonstrated during cycling trips where maintaining momentum uphill proves vital! If cyclists stop pedalling even momentarily whilst climbing a steep hill, they risk rolling backward faster than they were progressing forward through sheer determination alone.

I learned this principle during my rehabilitation after heart surgery. There were days when exercise seemed impossible, when the six stents in my heart felt like limitations rather than lifesavers. But I discovered that even minimal effort (perhaps just five minutes of gentle movement) kept the momentum going. Starting again after a complete stop would have been far more difficult.

This principle extends beyond physical pursuits; it applies equally across various aspects including diet changes or fitness routines built gradually over time without overwhelming oneself by trying everything simultaneously.

By embracing what I call "mini-midi-maxi" efforts tailored according to individual circumstances, we allow flexibility whilst ensuring continued progress:

Mini efforts:

On days when you're exhausted or time-constrained, do just the minimum: make one phone call instead of ten; do five minutes of exercise instead of thirty.

Midi efforts:

On regular days, maintain your standard activity level.

Maxi efforts:

On days when you feel particularly energetic or motivated, push beyond your usual limits.

This flexible approach prevents the all-or-nothing thinking that often derails goal achievement. During my Kilimanjaro training, there were days when I could only manage a short walk due to work commitments or fatigue. Rather than skipping exercise entirely, I'd take that walk, maintaining the habit and momentum that ultimately prepared me for the mountain.

Make It Social: Family Involvement

One thing about goal-setting is: don't keep it to yourself! Get your family involved as well. They're living this life with you, aren't they? Work together. Ask your children what goals they would like to achieve in the next year. Ask your partner, so it becomes a pooled activity where you're all working toward achieving your collective and individual goals.

When I was planning my career transition, I involved my family in the decision-making process. We discussed how it would affect our finances, our time together, and our future. This not only helped them understand the changes but also gave them ownership in the journey. My son set a goal to help me in the business to earn extra money, whilst my daughter wanted to attend one of my speaking engagements. These shared goals strengthened our bonds during a time of significant change.

I have a section on my phone where I note experiences that inspire me. During a conversation with someone who mentioned travelling on the Orient Express from London to Venice, I was captivated by their description. I envisioned arriving in Venice early in the morning, greeted by mist blanketing the iconic canals, whilst melodic calls of gondoliers echoed through narrow waterways. This enchanting idea captivated me so much that I immediately added it to my list of aspirations.

In contrast, when someone described their parachute jump experience, I knew without hesitation that this would NOT be making its way onto my goals list! The thought of intentionally jumping out of a perfectly functioning plane seemed perplexing to me. This illustrates how some aspirations resonate deeply whilst others do not connect at all.

Childlike Curiosity: Rediscovering Dreams

Working with children taught me valuable lessons about goal-setting. I'd visit Year Six classes at school and ask pupils about their Christmas lists; they would eagerly share items they wished for during the holiday season. Then I'd visit Year Three: seven-year-olds who seemed boundless when writing letters to Santa, enthusiastically producing endless lists of gifts they hoped he might deliver.

It's strange how these lists diminish as we get older, just as early dreams and ambitions are squashed when the realities of life kick in. We need to start dreaming again!

I saw this phenomenon in myself. After years in education, my dreams had narrowed to the next promotion, the next inspection result, the next budget cycle. Taking a step back and allowing myself to dream more broadly (about travel, about writing this book, about climbing Kilimanjaro) rekindled that childlike curiosity and expanded my sense of possibility.

Determining the specific goals you wish to achieve is a crucial step in the journey toward success and personal fulfilment.

Practical Implementation: The What-Where-When Formula

A couple of amazing books have clarified goal implementation for me. One standout title is James Clear's Atomic Habits, which delves into habit formation.

This book teaches you how to define:

What activities to engage in

Where these activities will take place

When they will occur

For instance, if I made a concrete plan to run for half an hour in Victoria Park right after I finish school each day, this specifies exactly:

What: Run for 30 minutes. **Where:** Victoria Park.

When: Immediately after school.

Such clarity eliminates ambiguity and allows mental preparation for the activity. Similarly, scheduling circuit training at my local gym during the six o'clock Tuesday class adheres to the same structured approach.

When preparing for Kilimanjaro, I applied this formula rigorously: What: Stair climber training for 45 minutes. Where: Local gym. When: 6:30 PM after work.

In addition to fitness goals, I apply this method to business development by making important telephone calls from my office between 9 to 12 after the children have gone to school. This organised method provides structure and infuses purpose into daily activities.

It's a simple yet effective system; if you commit yourself to being active whilst maintaining consistency with planned activities and remain clear about your intentions regarding where and when you'll execute them, it can make an extraordinary difference in successfully reaching your goals.

Beyond SMART: Redefining "Realistic"

Traditional methods for setting goals highlight the importance of adhering to the SMART criteria: Specific, Measurable, Attainable, Realistic, and Time-bound. However, an intriguing question arises: what constitutes "realistic" in goal-setting?

> "*Most people overestimate what they can do in one year and underestimate what they can do in ten years.*" – Bill Gates

When the Wright Brothers embarked on their quest for powered flight, many contemporaries dismissed their aspirations as unrealistic. Despite widespread scepticism, they persevered and succeeded in designing an aircraft capable of flight: a remarkable feat that changed transportation forever.

Similarly, Thomas Edison encountered countless failures whilst striving to invent the light bulb. At one time, illuminating a room with electric light was considered impossible by many.

In my own life, many would have considered it "unrealistic" for a troubled pupil sent to a special school to eventually become a headteacher. And later, climbing Kilimanjaro after heart surgery seemed equally unrealistic to many, including some medical professionals. But by redefining what's realistic based on my determination rather than conventional wisdom, I achieved both.

We must exercise caution when confining ourselves within conventional definitions of realism that may limit our potential. Instead of complicating goal-setting processes with overly intricate frameworks, maintain simplicity in task management through straightforward approaches toward achieving objectives.

The 1% Improvement Philosophy

Often, we believe that achieving our aspirations requires drastic changes in our lives or routines. However, during a recent talk by sports psychologist Jamil Qureshi (who has coached elite athletes across various sports) it was highlighted that instead of pursuing significant transformations, sometimes all it takes is a mere 1% tweak for meaningful improvement. If your goal is to enhance something by 100%, making just a 1% adjustment each day for an entire year can lead to remarkable progress.

A prime example of this philosophy can be seen through Dave Brailsford's leadership as the former director of the British cycling team at Sky. He adopted this incremental improvement strategy successfully by motivating every team member to seek enhancements within their specific areas by just 1%.

Prior to these changes, Great Britain had never secured an Olympic gold medal nor won the Tour de France as a nation. Yet after adopting this mindset during one Olympic cycle and Tour de France season, they achieved an unprecedented number of gold medals and celebrated their first victory in the Tour de France.

They focused on making small yet impactful improvements across various facets related to preparation and performance strategies:

The logistics team ensured consistency by transporting familiar bedding items for athletes to maintain sleep quality. Health team members sanitised door handles in accommodations meticulously to reduce illness exposure. Mechanics explored innovative designs aimed specifically at reducing bike weight.

All these seemingly minor adjustments collectively played a vital role in driving significant overall improvements for Team GB. This strategic approach enabled them to secure more gold medals than ever before and facilitated sustained success across two consecutive Olympic Games.

I applied this same philosophy when preparing for my career transition. Rather than attempting to master entrepreneurship overnight, I focused on improving my knowledge by just 1% each day: reading a few pages of a business book, practising one networking conversation, or learning one new digital skill. Over time, these small improvements accumulated into a substantial transformation.

Substantial achievements do not always necessitate radical overhauls; often it simply requires focusing on making small, yet effective tweaks directed toward continuous improvement over time.

Your Transformation Journey

As you work through the goal-setting process outlined in this chapter, remember that the true value lies not just in achieving your goals, but in who you become along the way. As Jim Rohn wisely noted in The Art of Exceptional Living, sometimes the person you develop into whilst pursuing your goals is the greatest reward of all.

Each step you take (each small victory, each setback overcome) shapes your character and expands your capacity. The discipline required to maintain consistency, the resilience developed through facing obstacles, and the wisdom gained from strategic planning all contribute to your personal evolution.

My own transformation from troubled pupil to educational leader to entrepreneur taught me this lesson repeatedly. The mindset I developed whilst overcoming educational challenges equipped me for leadership. The resilience built during my health crisis prepared me for career transition. Each goal achieved wasn't just an external milestone but an internal evolution.

Think of goal-setting as training for life itself. Just as an athlete develops strength, speed, and endurance through consistent practice, you're developing focus, determination, and adaptability through consistent goal pursuit. These qualities serve you not just in reaching your current objectives but in everything you undertake.

Key Takeaways

* **Start small:** Break down mountainous goals into manageable steps, focusing on the next action rather than the entire journey.
* **Connect emotionally:** Understand the "why" behind each goal; emotional connection provides the fuel for persistence when obstacles arise.
* **Visualise success:** Create visual reminders of what you're working toward to maintain motivation during challenging times.
* **Implement the What-Where-When formula:** Be specific about execution details to eliminate ambiguity and strengthen commitment.
* **Apply the 1% improvement approach:** Small, consistent improvements lead to remarkable results over time.
* **Involve others:** Share your goals with family members and create shared objectives to make the journey collaborative.
* **Maintain momentum:** Even minimal effort keeps you moving forward; complete stops make restarting much more difficult.
* **Challenge "realistic":** Don't let conventional thinking limit your aspirations; redefine realistic based on your determination.
* **Rediscover childlike curiosity:** Allow yourself to dream broadly again, expanding your sense of what's possible.

Actionable Steps

This week, create your personal "brain dump" of 100 goals. Set aside 30 minutes and write down everything you want to do, see, have, or become in your lifetime. Don't censor yourself; channel that Year Three child writing to Santa! Once complete, categorise these into 1-year, 3-year, 5-year, and 10-year timeframes, then select your top four from each category. For one of your 1-year goals, apply the What-Where-When formula: specify exactly what you'll do, where you'll do it, and when. This clarity will dramatically increase your likelihood of follow-through. Remember, you're not just setting goals; you're designing the life you want to live.

What You'll Learn in Chapter Four: From Classroom to Leadership

In Chapter four, you'll discover how my troubled educational start became the foundation for empathetic leadership. I'll share my journey from a special school for behavioural difficulties to becoming a headteacher, including the teachers who believed in me when no one else did and how their faith shaped my understanding of true leadership.

You'll learn the specific challenges of transitioning from classroom teacher to school leader, the practical skills required for managing people effectively, and how to make tough decisions whilst staying true to your values. I'll share real examples of difficult situations I faced, including budget crises that threatened jobs and how I navigated these challenges.

Most importantly, you'll discover how to create a culture where every person feels seen and valued, using practical strategies like the Achievement Gallery and the principles behind nurturing leadership that transforms both individuals and organisations.

CHAPTER FOUR

FROM CLASSROOM TO LEADERSHIP: EMBRACING GROWTH

One of the things that I was trying to develop during my time as a teacher was more experiential learning: creating opportunities for children to take an active part in their education rather than merely absorbing information. I firmly believed that children learn best when they're involved and making decisions, much like in business where you want to take your team forward, want them to have ownership of the approach rather than simply dictating what must be done.

UNITED States

Breaking Barriers: My Progression to Headship

I recall a particularly illuminating activity we undertook during my last year as a class teacher. We were exploring a topic called "Promises", and I found the prescribed curriculum rather uninspiring. I wanted to make it more exciting for the children, so I approached my colleague with an idea.

"Why don't we put on a wedding?" I suggested. "But we won't do the work; the children will. They'll be completely involved in every aspect."

She was rather sceptical at first. "But they're Year Six children," she protested. "They're not going to want to get married. They'll be embarrassed. They won't want to do something like that."

"Let's get them together and ask," I replied. And that's precisely what we did.

We gathered all sixty Year 6 children, and I posed a simple question: "Who has been to a wedding?" It turned out they knew weddings inside out. They listed everything involved in running a wedding: photographers, videographers, the person who gives the sermon, the evening disco, flower arrangements, wedding suits, bridesmaids' costumes, creating a comprehensive list of everything required.

Then I asked, "Who would like to get married?" To my colleague's surprise, nearly half the class raised their hands. I looked at her and said, "This is on."

The Wedding Project: Learning Through Experience

We created groups that met every Wednesday afternoon as part of their Religious Education lessons. Children selected different activities based on their interests: some worked on videography, others on photography, costumes and dresses, flower arrangements, or catering. Those who enjoyed writing were given the opportunity to compose speeches for the best man, the bridegroom, the bride, and even the sermon.

These children worked diligently on their projects. Some made arrangements to visit a local florist who showed them around, sharing ideas about what they could do. However, they soon discovered a significant challenge: costs. Hiring costumes, making a cake, arranging flowers; it all required money.

When they brought this problem to me, we opened up a new discussion: "How could we raise money?" They organised raffles and a sponsored walk, working towards a budget. Local businesses in our community generously supported the project, subsidising some of the costs.

For the first time in a long while, these children were truly engaged. The group working on flower arrangements, for instance, suddenly found themselves applying mathematics to budgets, even though some of them typically struggled with maths lessons. They worked on this project for several weeks, planning to hold the wedding at the end of the half term.

Their resourcefulness and creativity amazed me. They took detailed notes, made illustrations, and two pupils even designated themselves as "wedding planners". I remember finding one of these planners, a young lad, crying in the playground one afternoon.

"What's the matter? What's happened?" I asked him.

"I've just sorted out the seating arrangement and everyone's having a go at me because they don't want to sit there or next to certain people," he replied.

"Welcome to the real world," I told him. "You are the organiser. You stipulate where the seating will be, and they'll simply have to get along together." It was a genuine real-life experience for him.

The Big Day: When Planning Meets Reality

On the morning of the wedding, I was utterly astonished when a vintage car pulled up to our school to transport the bride and groom to the "church". The car belonged to one of the children's uncles who did this professionally, and he had volunteered his services. The bride and groom were taken for a ride around the block, around the roundabout, and back to the service.

CNO 876

What amazed me most was how everything went like clockwork. It was perfectly organised and timed, with everyone knowing exactly what they were supposed to be doing. This success stemmed from giving the children responsibility and ownership of the activity, allowing them to work to their strengths and develop multiple skills.

We held the service, took photographs, delivered messages and speeches, and even invited the local bowls club (who had been teaching the children crown green bowls that half term) as special guests. They arrived in their blazers, sat at each table, and interacted wonderfully with the children.

I wouldn't say the food was Michelin-starred (for health and safety reasons, it was mostly pre-packaged), but it was beautifully presented. The children even organised a disco with carefully selected music, working out how long each track would last to create a timed production schedule for the entire wedding.

We created a commemorative book and video that remained in the school foyer for many years until someone (presumably) took it as a memento. This event took place about 18 years ago. During lockdown, I decided to sift through some of the photographs that were taken and created a video of the event, which I shared as a YouTube link with the former pupils. It spread like wildfire, bringing back wonderful memories for these now-adult pupils.

Creating a School with Vision

Reflecting on my time as a headteacher and how this approach can be adapted to business, I recall my first session with staff after leaving the classroom behind. I walked into an office (not a staffroom full of teachers, but a solitary office with just myself) and my primary concern was creating a school with an exciting curriculum, where children and staff had a genuine voice in school operations.

"I know that the school has great potential," I remember thinking, "but unlocking the vision that I want to see in place will require a lot of effort and teamwork."

Not everyone agreed with my vision initially. It was sometimes quite challenging to implement these ideas, and we were careful not to change things too rapidly, as that could create chaos. Some staff had different opinions, and discussions occasionally got heated.

Teamwork proved essential when trying to transform ideas into amazing results, much like designing an iPhone, I suppose. Building a great school isn't about rigidly adhering to one fixed plan; it's about refining and improving as new insights emerge.

In addition to launching initiatives, I found myself juggling countless ideas whilst constantly adapting to each new challenge: how to engage children, support teachers, strengthen the school community, and involve parents. Some ideas worked brilliantly, whilst others needed refining, but unexpected solutions often emerged through this process of trial, discussion, and collaboration. This is where real transformation happens.

The Rock Tumbler Analogy

I'm reminded of a wonderful analogy shared by Steve Jobs that perfectly illustrates this concept. He recounted how, as a child, he had a neighbour with a rock tumbler: a simple canister powered by a motor. They gathered rough stones, added grit and liquid, and switched it on. The rock tumbler churned noisily, and everything seemed rather chaotic, but when they opened it the next day, the once ordinary stones had been transformed into beautifully polished gems.

That's exactly how our school developed over the subsequent years. At first, change felt somewhat messy. Staff had differing opinions, and discussions occasionally became heated. But like those rocks in the tumbler, we refined each other through collaboration, sharpening our approach and strengthening our school. By embracing this process, we didn't merely make minor improvements; we transformed the school into something truly exciting, where learning methods evolved, and children became actively involved in their education.

As I reflect on running a school, and how this can be adapted to business contexts, the central theme remains the same: true transformation happens when people work together to refine ideas, even when the process seems messy at first. We were learning by doing, and the children were at the heart of this approach.

Leadership Lessons in Business

When I consider how this translates to my current business, I appreciate how the company brings partners together, encouraging them to collaborate on tasks and generate ideas. I love that the partners in our company have ownership; it's not a case of "corporate versus workers", but truly a team effort.

I recall visiting our main business headquarters in London: a massive building in Colindale housing 1,700 staff. Whilst using the lift system one day, I noticed a sign asking people for ideas to improve customer service and partner development. Anyone who submitted ideas would be invited to "Piggy Den" (our logo at the time was a pig).

The remarkable thing was that these contributors could be anyone: a porter, a cleaner, a catering staff member, not just executives. The company recognised that with 1,700 staff, someone somewhere would have a brilliant idea. Those selected would present their ideas directly to the CEO, chairman, and finance director. I loved the concept that a cleaner might propose a fantastic idea for improving customer service, or a car park attendant might suggest ways to develop partners more effectively.

The reward for having an idea selected? A weekend trip to New York with a partner, all expenses paid. What brilliant thinking! It rewarded people for engaging and sharing ideas, demonstrating that everyone's voice in the organisation could be heard. It took my breath away.

Leading Through Crisis: The COVID Experience

Nowhere was leadership more powerfully demonstrated than during the COVID pandemic when the world essentially shut down. Prior to the lockdowns, the company I worked for mobilised with remarkable speed. Someone had this vision of what could happen, and they got their teams working really quickly.

They purchased laptops and established systems allowing staff to work from home whilst remaining connected through communication platforms. I'm not sure how they managed to do that so rapidly, but what happened when lockdown kicked in was truly impressive.

When the company needed to close its physical locations, people could still call in and be looked after by the support team. As partners in the field, we could no longer go out and meet people face-to-face because of the risks involved, but what the company did through inspired leadership was create a virtual and remote system.

This allowed us to connect with potential customers and showcase our products and services without putting anyone in danger. The system also enabled new people to join our organisation (many who had been turned down by their workplaces or had lost their jobs) to be trained, supported, and mentored through the process.

Our business actually flourished during that period. That was inspired leadership: someone with the vision to anticipate possibilities, rise to challenges, and find ways to continue moving forward. That system remains in use today for training purposes and has expanded to cover other products as well.

The pandemic also saw the widespread adoption of tools like Zoom, which became essential for maintaining connections during those challenging two years. By embracing technology and adapting quickly, we not only survived but thrived. This experience showed me that true leadership means not just reacting to a crisis, but preparing for it and finding opportunities within it.

The Evolution of Leadership Understanding

What strikes me most about my journey from classroom teacher to headteacher, and now in business, is how my understanding of leadership has evolved. In the early days, I thought leadership meant having all the answers, being the person at the front directing others. But I learned that true leadership is quite different.

Leadership is about creating an environment where others can do their best work. It's about asking the right questions rather than always providing answers. It's about empowering people to take ownership and make decisions, just like those Year 6 children planning their wedding.

The wedding project taught me that when people (regardless of age) are given real responsibility and ownership, they rise to meet it. They become creative, resourceful, and surprisingly capable. This principle has guided every leadership role I've held since.

Systems and Structures That Enable Success

One thing I learned as a headteacher is that good leadership creates systems and structures that enable success, even in challenging circumstances. The COVID response demonstrated this perfectly. The company didn't just react to the crisis; they had anticipated the need for flexible working arrangements and had systems in place that could be rapidly deployed.

This taught me that part of leadership is thinking ahead, anticipating challenges, and building resilience into your systems. It's not enough to lead when things are going well; true leadership is tested when everything seems to be falling apart.

In education, this meant having systems that could adapt when a key teacher was absent, when unexpected events disrupted the schedule, or when new government requirements changed our approach. In business, it means having processes that can function remotely, training programmes that can be delivered virtually, and communication systems that keep everyone connected regardless of physical location.

The Importance of Inclusive Leadership

One of the most powerful lessons from the "Piggy Den" initiative was about inclusive leadership. The idea that great ideas can come from anyone, regardless of their position in the hierarchy, revolutionised my thinking about organisational structure.

In schools, I started asking the cleaning staff about what they observed during their work. They often had insights about which areas were being underutilised, which classrooms had problems, or how the flow of people through the building could be improved. Their perspective was invaluable because they saw the school from a completely different angle.

In my business, I learned to listen to newer team members who brought fresh perspectives, especially younger partners, many of whom communicated through the world of social media, and our customers who experienced our services in ways we hadn't anticipated.

True leadership means creating space for all voices to be heard and valued.

From Control to Empowerment

Perhaps the biggest shift in my leadership journey was moving from a control-based approach to an empowerment-based one. Early in my career, I thought effective leadership meant having tight control over every aspect of an operation. But the wedding project showed me something different.

When I stepped back and let the children take real ownership, they achieved things I never could have mandated or controlled into existence. They found resources I didn't know existed, solved problems I hadn't anticipated, and created solutions that were better than anything I could have prescribed.

This principle applies directly to business leadership. When team members have genuine ownership of their work, when they understand the vision and are trusted to find their own way to contribute to it, the results often exceed what any top-down directive could achieve.

Key Takeaways

* **Leadership is a mindset, not a title:** True leadership involves empowering others and creating environments where people can thrive.

* **Experiential learning drives engagement:** People learn and grow more when they have ownership and real responsibility.

* **Embrace the messy process of transformation:** Like rocks in a tumbler, refinement through collaboration creates better results than rigid plans.

* **Great ideas can come from anywhere:** Inclusive leadership values input from all levels of an organisation.

* **Systems and structures enable success:** Good leadership anticipates challenges and builds resilient processes.

* **Crisis reveals true leadership:** The best leaders don't just react to problems; they prepare for them and find opportunities within them.

* **Empowerment beats control:** When people have genuine ownership, they often achieve more than what can be mandated.

* **Leadership is about asking questions, not having all the answers:** The best leaders create space for others to contribute their expertise.

Actionable Steps

Identify one leadership quality you'd like to develop further this week. Choose from: empathy and active listening, strategic thinking and vision-setting, building and empowering teams, adaptability and resilience, communication and inspiration, or decision-making under pressure. Write down three specific actions you can take in the next seven days to strengthen this quality. For example, if you choose empathy and active listening, you might: 1) Have a conversation with a colleague where you ask questions and listen without offering solutions, 2) Observe a meeting and notice whose voices aren't being heard, 3) Ask someone in your team about their biggest current challenge and really listen to their response. Remember, leadership is a skill that develops through deliberate practice and continuous learning. Whether you're currently in a formal leadership position or not, these qualities will serve you well in any role or situation.

What's Coming in Chapter Five: Creating Ethical Exit Strategies

In our next chapter, we'll explore the emotional and practical challenges of building alternative income streams whilst maintaining your professional integrity. You'll discover how I managed the transition from the security of education to creating financial options through a side business.

We'll examine the ethical considerations of pursuing opportunities outside your primary career, how to balance competing commitments, and the importance of creating choices for yourself before you need them. You'll learn valuable strategies for building something part-time that could eventually provide full-time security, and gain insights from the early days of developing a business alongside a demanding teaching career.

Chapter Five will equip you with practical tools for assessing opportunities, maintaining professional boundaries, and most importantly, how to start building your own ethical exit strategy. For those considering additional income streams, planning for career transitions, or simply seeking more security and options in their professional life, this chapter will provide both inspiration and practical guidance to help you move forward with confidence and integrity.

CHAPTER FIVE
CREATING ETHICAL EXIT STRATEGIES

A mentor I often listened to in those early years was Jim Rohn. He became a kind of anchor for me, a voice of perspective and possibility. I remember him saying, in sharing his own story: "Work full-time on your job and part-time on your fortune." That really stuck with me.

It made sense, because at that point, that's all I could do. I started my side gig very part-time, with whatever time I could spare. When you're a deputy headteacher with a full schedule of responsibilities, you don't exactly have abundant free time. But that's precisely the point: we rarely find time; we have to make it.

Building the Side Business

From the start, I understood the importance of setting goals to keep myself on track. One of those goals was crystal clear: to step away from the stress of being a deputy headteacher and eventually a headteacher, by the age of 50. I'd made that decision years before, and when I began my side venture, I was hopeful. That was all I had at first: hope.

But over time, through attending events, conferences, and getting around people who were already succeeding, that hope began to shift. It turned into belief. As the income started to come in and the business began to grow, that belief became a driving force so strong it wouldn't let me stop.

This transformation from hope to belief to certainty is perhaps the most valuable part of creating an exit strategy. When you start, you hope it might work. As you see small successes, you begin to believe it's possible. And eventually, that belief becomes so strong it transforms into certainty: a knowing that you've created real options for yourself.

The Ant Philosophy: Preparing for Winter

It required commitment. Late nights. Weekends. And I always remembered Jim Rohn's "ant philosophy": Why do ants work so hard in the summer? Because winter is coming. During my "summers" (evenings, weekends, holidays), I worked as much as I could. And sure enough, my "winter" came when I faced serious health issues. But by then, I had created choices because I'd made those early decisions.

I also began reading a lot of personal-development books. I used to say at team events: The things you want to reach in life? Sometimes you get there by standing on the books you've read. The lessons become your foundation.

One of the most important lessons I've learned is this: to become financially free, the greatest value is not just in what you gain, it's in who you become along the journey.

The real investment wasn't money. It was time. And time, as we all know, is one of your most valuable assets.

The Power of Association

I made sure I got around good people. Jim Rohn famously said, "You become the average of the five people you spend the most time with." The one thing I already had was a hunger for change. I wanted to spend more time with my family. I shared earlier that, as a child, I rarely saw my dad. He left when I was young, and it wasn't until much later that we reconnected. I didn't want to repeat that story. I wanted to be present for my family in a way my father couldn't be for me.

I also wanted to travel. Up to that point, my travel had mostly consisted of school trips: cold corridors, noisy hallways, yelling at kids to get back in their rooms. Not quite the dream. I wanted to explore the world on my own terms, to see places I'd only read about in books or seen in films.

Prioritising What Matters

So I planned. I used what little time was left in the day, and I worked. I carved out those "spare" time slots, although let's be honest, spare time doesn't really exist. You have to prioritise. I made choices. I gave up golf for a while, not because I didn't enjoy it, but because I knew I needed that time to grow my business.

Still, there were moments I felt guilty. That complex so many educators have: if we're not giving every single minute of ourselves to the job, we're somehow failing. It's a demanding career. Evenings filled with marking. Weekends lost to report-writing. The paperwork and bureaucracy were killing me. It wasn't just the job; it was the total ownership it had over my time.

That only fuelled my fire.

The Ethical Dilemma

I kept things quiet. I didn't make a big noise about what I was doing. I was afraid of criticism, worried people would question my commitment to teaching, even though that commitment was never in doubt. I wanted to improve education. I wanted to change how we developed young minds.

But I'd seen too much. I'd seen teachers burned out. I'd seen people suffer silently, some to the point of taking their own lives. One close friend of mine did. And I realised something important: when you're on half pay or struggling with your health, the people criticising you won't be the ones paying your bills.

So I kept doing my job. I honoured my role. But I weaved my side gig into evenings and weekends. Quietly. Consistently. Part-time.

That little side hobby? It paid off big time. It turned out to be one of the best decisions of my life.

The Ethics of Creating an Exit Strategy

Many educators feel trapped in their careers. The pension, the security, the familiarity: these become golden handcuffs that keep us locked into positions, even when they're no longer serving us. But there's nothing unethical about creating options for yourself.

The key is to maintain your integrity throughout the process:

Never let your side venture interfere with your primary responsibilities. I was scrupulous about this. During school hours, I was 100% present for my pupils and staff.

Be honest but discreet. I never lied about what I was doing, but I also didn't broadcast it to those who might misunderstand my intentions.

Recognise that creating financial security actually makes you a better educator. When you're not stressed about money, you can be more present and effective in your role.

The Freedom Timeline: When to Make Your Move

Creating an exit strategy isn't about abandoning ship as quickly as possible. It's about creating choice and freedom on your own timeline. Here's how I approached it:

Set clear financial targets. I needed to replace my headteacher's salary before I could consider leaving. I calculated exactly what that meant in monthly income from my side business.

Create a three-to-five-year plan. I didn't expect overnight success. I gave myself adequate time to build something sustainable.

Test before you leap. Once my side income started approaching my salary, I considered taking a sabbatical to test the waters before making a permanent decision.

Have adequate savings. I built a cushion of at least six months' expenses before making any major changes.

Consider a phased transition. Some colleagues have reduced to part-time teaching whilst growing their businesses.

Balancing Guilt and Growth

The guilt I mentioned earlier is common amongst educators. We're drawn to this profession because we care deeply about making a difference. Pursuing something outside of education can feel like betrayal.

But here's what I've learned: Your value as an educator isn't measured by your martyrdom. Taking care of yourself (financially, physically, emotionally) isn't selfish. It's necessary. I've seen too many brilliant teachers burn out, becoming shells of their former enthusiastic selves. What good does that do for pupils? By creating options for myself, I ensured that the time I did spend in education was quality time. I was present, energetic, and motivated: not running on fumes.

The Unexpected Benefits

What surprised me most about building a side business wasn't just the financial rewards. It was how the skills I developed made me a better educator and leader:

Better time management. When you have limited hours to build something, you become ruthlessly efficient with your time.

Enhanced communication skills. My business required me to become better at explaining complex ideas simply: a skill that translated directly to the classroom.

Broader perspective. Engaging with the world outside of education gave me fresh insights to bring back to my school.

Renewed passion. Having an outlet for other interests actually rekindled my love for education, rather than diminishing it.

More empathy for pupils. Putting myself in the vulnerable position of learning something new helped me relate better to my pupils' struggles.

The Reality of the Part-Time Journey

Let me be clear: building something on the side isn't easy. There were nights I fell asleep at my desk, weekends when I missed family outings, and moments of doubt when I questioned if it was all worth it.

But I approached it with discipline and consistency. I didn't need to work 40 extra hours a week; I just needed to work a focused 10-15 hours on the right things.

Think of it like compound interest. Small, consistent efforts, applied intelligently over time, yield remarkable results. Five years might seem like a long time when you're starting, but it will pass whether you build something or not. The question is: where do you want to be when those five years have elapsed?

Ethical Considerations and Boundaries

Staying Grounded Whilst Building Something New

Over time, I came to value the importance of keeping things clear, not because I did everything perfectly, but because clarity brings confidence. It also protects the trust you've worked hard to earn.

Key Lessons for Creating Your Own Ethical Exit Strategy

Looking back on my journey from stressed deputy headteacher to someone with options, these are the key lessons I'd share:

Start where you are. You don't need perfect conditions to begin. Start small, with whatever time and resources you have available.

Leverage your existing skills. As educators, we have valuable, transferable skills: communication, leadership, organisation, empathy. These are gold in many other fields.

Find mentors who are where you want to be. Books, podcasts, and actual relationships with people who have walked this path are invaluable.

Protect your primary income whilst building your second. Never jeopardise your current position until your new venture is proven and stable.

Remember why you're doing this. For me, it was about family time, travel, and freedom from stress. Your "why" will keep you going when motivation wanes.

The Psychological Shift

This psychological shift is powerful. It changes how you carry yourself, how you make decisions, how you view challenges. You move from feeling trapped to feeling empowered. From reacting to circumstances to creating them.

When you have options, everything changes. The difficult parent meeting becomes less stressful because you're not desperate to keep your job. The unreasonable demands from leadership lose their power because you know you have alternatives. The Sunday-evening dread that many educators experience begins to fade because you're building something that excites you.

And that's a gift that extends far beyond the financial rewards.

Actionable Steps to Begin Your Exit Strategy

Ready to create your own ethical exit strategy? Here are concrete steps to get started:

Conduct a skills audit. List all your transferable skills. Which ones could be valuable in other contexts?

Identify potential ventures that align with your strengths. What could you do that would leverage your existing capabilities whilst building new ones?

Allocate specific time blocks. Schedule 5-10 hours each week dedicated to your side venture. Treat these as non-negotiable appointments with yourself.

Join communities of like-minded professionals. Find groups who are building alternative income streams. Their support will be invaluable.

Set clear, staged goals. What do you want to achieve in three months? Six months? One year? Make these specific and measurable.

Track your progress. Keep a journal of your journey: the challenges, the wins, the lessons. This will become a valuable resource as you grow.

Invest in your knowledge. Allocate a budget for books, courses, and mentorship in your chosen field.

The Long-Term Vision

Creating an exit strategy isn't about escaping your job; it's about creating choice. Some people build alternative income streams and choose to stay in their current role because they love it, but now they do it from a position of choice rather than necessity.
Others, like me, eventually transition out of education into new adventures. Both paths are valid. The key is having options.

Your exit strategy might lead you back to education with renewed passion, or it might open doors to opportunities you never imagined. Either way, you'll be making decisions from a position of strength rather than fear.

Key Takeaways

* **Work full-time on your job, part-time on your future:** Your current position deserves your best, but your future deserves your investment too.

* **Prepare for winter during summer:** Build alternative options whilst things are stable, so you're prepared when challenges come.

* **Track your mindset journey:** Hope to belief to certainty alongside your practical achievements.

* **Time, not money, is your most valuable investment:** How you allocate your hours ultimately determines your options.

* **Creating options isn't disloyal to education:** You can remain committed to your role whilst building alternatives.

* **Choose your influences wisely:** You become the average of the five people you spend the most time with.

* **Small, consistent efforts compound over time:** You don't need massive action; you need consistent action in the right direction.

* **Maintain ethical boundaries:** Never compromise your professional integrity whilst building your exit strategy.

Actionable Steps

This week, conduct a personal skills audit and identify one potential side venture that aligns with your strengths and interests. List all your transferable skills from education (communication, leadership, organisation, problem-solving, empathy, etc.). Then research one business opportunity or income stream that could leverage these skills. Allocate two hours this weekend to explore this opportunity further: read about it, watch videos, or speak to someone already doing it. Remember, you're not committing to anything yet; you're simply exploring possibilities. The goal is to move from "someday I might" to "here's one specific thing I could actually do." Your future self will thank you for taking this first step towards creating options.

What's Coming in Chapter 6: Understanding Fear & Overcoming It

In the next chapter, we'll explore one of the most universal experiences, fear, and how it often stands between us and our next breakthrough.

You'll learn how fear shaped my decisions early on, how I began challenging my comfort zone, and the unexpected lessons I picked up along the way.

From confronting childhood insecurities to facing adult responsibilities head-on, this chapter will give you a real look at what it takes to move forward, even when fear is whispering that you can't.

If you've ever felt like fear was keeping you small, Chapter 6 will give you both the perspective and practical tools to start pushing back.

CHAPTER SIX

UNDERSTANDING FEAR AND OVERCOMING IT

Fear had always been my constant companion during my teaching career. Not the healthy kind that keeps you alert and prepared, but the paralysing sort that whispers doubts about your worth and capabilities. It was particularly loud during those early days when I was juggling my teaching responsibilities with other pursuits, constantly worried about what colleagues might think.

As I mentioned in the previous chapter, I'd often worry about what people thought of me, not giving 100% of my time to the job, having other things going on in my life. But that's normal. It's healthy. And it shouldn't be looked down upon.

Still, the concern lingered, until someone shared this with me: "What people think about you is absolutely none of your business."

That struck a chord. What is important is what you think about yourself, your responsibilities to your family, and the dreams you want to pursue.

The Fear of Not Being Enough

Against all odds, I was appointed headteacher of the school. There had been opposition; people questioned my commitment. "He has a side gig, you know..." The fear of being judged as insufficiently dedicated nearly stopped me from applying altogether.

But I'd made a decision: I wasn't going to let that fear stop me.

During the interview, I didn't focus on defending my time or apologising for my other interests. Instead, I focused on my vision: to create a school, a community, where children had a voice and a say in their own learning. I poured everything I had into that moment. Years of personal development. Years of passion. It was the best performance of my life.

The fear hadn't disappeared, but I had learned to act despite it. This distinction would prove crucial in everything that followed.

Understanding the Nature of Fear

Fear operates on multiple levels, and understanding these can help us respond more effectively. There's the immediate, visceral fear: the racing heart when you're about to give a presentation. Then there's the deeper, more insidious fear: the one that questions your fundamental worth and capability.

I had always wanted to run a school. That dream was born from my own poor experience in education. I knew I could do better by fostering experiential learning, not just chalk and talk or ensuring handwriting was tidy. But fear told me I wasn't qualified enough, experienced enough, traditional enough.

The reality was different. I wanted to build pupils' self-esteem. I wanted staff to take a genuine interest in every child's passions and talents. I even created an Achievement Gallery: a space celebrating pupils doing what they loved: sailing, go-karting, rugby, chess. If they were passionate about it, we showcased it. Fear had tried to convince me that my unconventional approach was wrong. But when I looked at the results (engaged pupils, improved relationships, a stronger sense of community), I realised that fear had been lying to me.

The Susan Boyle Revelation

Then came my first INSET day, staff training. I wanted to make an impact, but I was also terrified. What if my message didn't resonate? What if the staff thought I was naïve or overly idealistic?

I decided to share the story of Susan Boyle.

You know it. A seemingly frumpy woman steps onto the stage of Britain's Got Talent. Simon Cowell and Amanda Holden roll their eyes. The pre-judging look she received will forever be etched in my mind. Then she opens her mouth and the entire room changes. Their jaws dropped as her beautiful voice filled the space.

I paused the video and turned to my staff. My heart was racing, but I pushed through the fear and said these words:

"The real crime here isn't that they judged her before she sang. The real crime is that Susan Boyle went through nursery, primary, secondary, even tertiary education and not one single person spotted her gift."

That day, I gave them a mission, despite my fear of seeming too demanding or unrealistic: "Don't let a single child go through your class this year without discovering their passions. Find out what they love. What they do in their spare time. What makes them light up."

The Fear of Being Vulnerable

Sharing that story required vulnerability. I was essentially telling my staff that our entire education system had failed Susan Boyle, and by extension, countless other children. I was asking them to see beyond academic results and test scores to the human beings in their care.

Fear whispered that this was too soft, too touchy-feely for a school environment. But I pushed through because I knew it mattered.

And they did respond. We wove their pupils' passions into our awards assemblies. I interviewed children about what made them tick. We showed slides of them in action, doing what they loved. It gave me something to connect with them over. Even when a pupil had behavioural issues, I could sit with them and say, "Tell me about your music," or "How's the chess going?"

That changed the dynamic. It strengthened relationships. It built a sense of community. And it raised self-esteem, not just in the pupils, but in the staff too. It opened people up.

The Business Lesson in Fear

This experience taught me something profound that I would later apply in business: We're often told to "close" people. But actually, we need to do the opposite. We need to open them up. Fear tells us to keep our cards close to our chest, to maintain professional distance, to avoid showing interest in case it's seen as weakness. But the reality is quite different.

We need to ask questions, show interest, and mean it. When we demonstrate genuine care for others (their passions, their struggles, their dreams), they become more willing to engage with us.
Because, as the saying goes: "People don't care how much you know until they know how much you care."

Fear vs Danger: The Critical Distinction

One of the most important lessons I learned during this period was distinguishing between fear and actual danger. When I was worried about people questioning my commitment because of my other interests, I was experiencing fear. But was there actual danger?

The worst that could happen was criticism or judgement. Uncomfortable, yes. Dangerous, no.

When I was nervous about sharing the Susan Boyle story with my staff, I was afraid they might think I was naïve. But the actual danger was minimal. The worst case would be some eye-rolling or scepticism. The best case (which is what happened) was a transformation in how we approached education.

This distinction is crucial. Fear often masquerades as prudence or common sense, but it's frequently just our brain's way of keeping us in our comfort zone. Learning to recognise when you're dealing with fear rather than genuine danger can be liberating.

The Ripple Effect of Courage

What happened after that first staff training was remarkable. When I showed courage in being vulnerable, in sharing an unconventional message, it gave others permission to do the same.

Teachers began sharing their own stories and passions with pupils. They started incorporating more creative approaches into their lessons. The Achievement Gallery became a source of pride for the entire school community.

Fear had told me that stepping out of traditional educational approaches would lead to chaos or criticism. Instead, it led to connection and growth.

Strategies for Working with Fear

Through this experience and many others since, I've developed several approaches for dealing with fear:

1 Acknowledge It Without Judgement

Fear isn't wrong or weak. It's human. When I felt nervous about that staff training, I didn't pretend the fear wasn't there. I acknowledged it: "I'm nervous about this presentation. That's normal."

2 Examine the Evidence

I asked myself: "What evidence do I have that this will go badly?" Usually, the answer was "none" or "very little." Fear often operates on assumptions rather than facts.

3 Consider the Cost of Inaction

What would happen if I let fear win? In the case of the Susan Boyle story, the cost would be maintaining a status quo that wasn't serving our pupils well. That cost was higher than the risk of some temporary discomfort.

4 Start with Small Acts of Courage

I didn't begin my headteacher role by completely revolutionising the school overnight. I started with small changes, building confidence with each success.

5 Connect with Your Deeper Purpose

My fear of judgement was real, but my commitment to creating a better educational experience for children was stronger. When fear and purpose clash, let purpose win.

Fear as Information

Over time, I've learned to see fear differently. Rather than an enemy to be defeated, it's information to be processed. Fear often tells us that something matters to us. If I hadn't cared deeply about education and those children's futures, I wouldn't have felt afraid about getting it wrong.

The presence of fear can actually be a good sign: it means you're pushing beyond your comfort zone, attempting something that matters to you.

The Long-Term View

Years later, I can see how overcoming that fear during my first staff training set the tone for my entire tenure as headteacher. It established me as someone willing to challenge conventional thinking, someone who cared more about pupil outcomes than appearing traditionally professional.

This reputation served me well when I later made the transition to business. People knew I was someone who would act on principle rather than just follow the crowd.

Opening People Up

That phrase, "opening people up," has become central to how I approach all relationships, whether in education or business. Fear encourages us to close down, to protect ourselves, to maintain barriers. Courage invites us to open up, to show genuine interest in others, to be vulnerable when appropriate.
The pupils whose passions we celebrated didn't just feel more engaged with school. They felt seen and valued as complete human beings. The staff didn't just become better teachers. They became better at connecting with the young people in their care.

This principle applies everywhere. In business, instead of trying to manipulate or pressure people into decisions, I focus on understanding what they truly want and need. Instead of presenting a facade of perfection, I'm willing to share my own struggles and uncertainties.

Fear tells us this approach is risky. Experience has taught me it's actually the foundation of all meaningful success.

Key Takeaways

* **What others think of you is none of your business:** Focus on your own values and responsibilities rather than seeking universal approval.

* **Fear often masquerades as prudence:** Learn to distinguish between genuine danger and fear-based hesitation.

* **Vulnerability can be a strength:** Sharing authentic concerns and passions often creates stronger connections than maintaining professional distance.

* **Small acts of courage build confidence:** You don't need to revolutionise everything at once; start with manageable challenges.

* **Fear indicates something matters to you:** The presence of fear often signals that you're pursuing something important.

* **Opening people up beats closing them down:** Show genuine interest in others' passions and struggles rather than trying to control or manipulate.

Actionable Steps

Identify one fear that's currently holding you back from connecting more authentically with someone in your life (whether a colleague, pupil, family member, or friend). This might be fear of seeming unprofessional, fear of judgement, or fear of vulnerability. Today, take one small action to "open them up" rather than keeping them at a distance. Ask about their interests, share something genuine about yourself, or acknowledge a struggle you're both facing. Notice how this changes the dynamic between you, and use that insight to guide future interactions. Remember: people don't care how much you know until they know how much you care.

What's Coming in Chapter 7: Health and wellbeing during change

In the next chapter, we'll explore one of the most physically and mentally demanding challenges I've ever faced, climbing Mount Kilimanjaro. But this story is really about what the climb taught me about **health, wellbeing, and listening to your body.**

You'll learn how I prepared for the mountain by first taking responsibility for my health, making lifestyle changes after a major wake-up call, and committing to a level of physical and mental endurance I never thought possible.

This chapter will inspire you to treat your health as your most valuable asset. If you've been pushing your limits or ignoring warning signs, Chapter 7 will encourage you to pause, reset, and start climbing toward a healthier, more balanced life, one step at a time.

CHAPTER SEVEN
HEALTH AND WELLBEING DURING CHANGE

I've chosen to share the part of my journey that focuses on recovery and working with health coaches. The truth is simple: your health is your wealth. For many years, I was relentlessly driven to create wealth, to give my family and me more choices. But in doing so, I neglected my own personal wellbeing. I grabbed food on the go, worked late nights repeatedly, and rarely took breaks on weekends. This routine continued, year after year.

It was a recipe for disaster.

The Price of Relentless Pursuit

Looking back, the warning signs were everywhere. I did little exercise, perhaps the occasional round of golf, but nothing consistent. My days were consumed with work, my evenings filled with more work, and my weekends became just another opportunity to catch up on what I hadn't finished during the week.

I told myself this was temporary. I convinced myself that once I reached a certain level of success, I'd slow down, take better care of myself, spend more quality time with my family. But that day never seemed to arrive. There was always another goal, another target, another mountain to climb in my professional life.

The irony wasn't lost on me. I was working tirelessly to create a better life for my family, but in the process, I was jeopardising my ability to actually enjoy that life with them.

Resigning from my stressful job brought relief, but also a painful realisation: At what cost? And it's at that moment of relief that you're often at your most vulnerable. The adrenaline that had been carrying me for years suddenly stopped, and I was left to confront the damage I'd done to my body and mind.

I asked myself: what was all that effort for?

The Wake-Up Call

That question became even sharper when the surgeon pointed to the screen, showing the blockages in my arteries. It's not until you're faced with your own mortality that you truly understand how vital your health is.

The images on that screen told a story I didn't want to acknowledge. Years of stress, poor nutrition, lack of exercise, and relentless pressure had taken their toll. My body had been sending me signals for months, perhaps years, but I'd been too busy, too focused on external achievements to listen.

Following the insertion of six stents, I was told how lucky I'd been. Many people don't get a second chance. And I didn't want to waste mine.

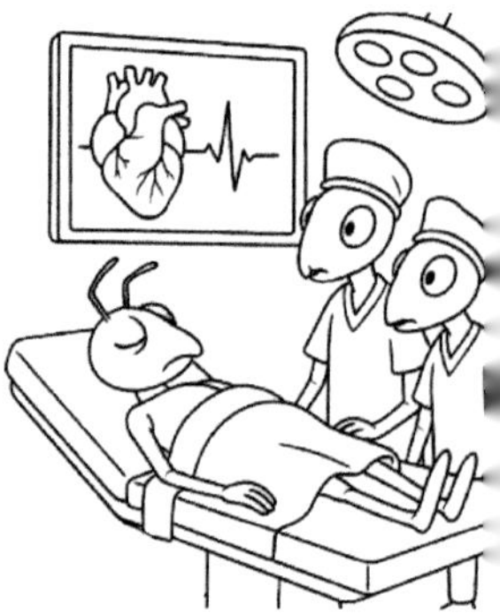

Life isn't about what happens to you; it's about how you respond to it. Standing in that hospital, with my chest still tender from the procedure, I made a decision that would change everything. I decided I had a lot of living left to do.

The Decision to Change

With the "plumbing" fixed, it was time to fix my mindset and change my lifestyle. Why? Because I want to be around when my children grow up. I want to be there for my future grandchildren and be able to get up off the floor unaided after building a Duplo or Lego creation with them.

This wasn't about vanity or wanting to look good in photographs. This was about longevity, about being present for the moments that truly matter. I realised that all the wealth I'd been chasing would be meaningless if I wasn't healthy enough to enjoy it with the people I love.

The medical intervention had given me a reprieve, but I knew that real change would require a complete transformation in how I approached my health and wellbeing.

Meeting the Game-Changers

That's when I brought in two people who helped change my life.

Owen Phillips: The Physical Transformation

Owen Phillips was a personal trainer who would become instrumental in my recovery. Owen had actually worked with my friend Huw, the headteacher who sadly took his own life. Huw introduced me to Owen, and I'll always be grateful for that connection.

Owen ran his own gym and was a living example of what consistent fitness could achieve. His appearance was striking evidence of the benefits of regular exercise. You could immediately see the results of his dedication to health and fitness. He approached fitness with a philosophy that resonated with me, understanding that sustainable change happens gradually, through consistency rather than dramatic short-term efforts. This was exactly what I needed to hear.

Owen helped me get into shape, supporting me through a two-year transformation that saw me lose nearly 20 kilos. The process wasn't always easy. There were days when I felt too tired, too busy, or too discouraged to continue. But Owen's approach was patient and persistent. He helped me understand that consistency was key.

The physical changes were obvious, but the mental changes were equally important. As I became stronger physically, I found myself more resilient mentally. The discipline required for regular exercise began to spill over into other areas of my life, creating a positive cycle of improvement.

Tristan Lee: The Mindset Revolution

The second person who changed my life was Tristan Lee, my wellbeing coach. I met Tristan at a conference where he was speaking about self-care and its importance in building a strong business.

Tristan looks 25, but he's actually in his 50's. I remember walking up to him afterward and saying, "I don't know what you're doing, but I want to do it." That was nearly ten a decade ago, and we still work together today.

Tristan helped me hugely with nutrition and mindset. Under his guidance, I became plant-based and started eating what I consider real food. This wasn't about following the latest diet trend; it was about understanding how nutrition affects every aspect of our lives, from energy levels to mental clarity to emotional stability.

The combination of Owen's physical training programme and Tristan's nutritional guidance created a transformation that went far beyond what I'd expected. I had more energy, more vitality, and this massively impacted my business too.

But perhaps most importantly, Tristan helped me recognise my self-worth. He reminded me that, regardless of accolades or achievements, we are all good enough. This was a profound shift for someone who had spent years tying his value to external validation and professional success.

The Ripple Effect

The impact of these changes extended far beyond my personal health. I was so impressed with Owen and Tristan's approaches that I even invited both of them to speak at a regional conference I organised, so others could benefit from their messages too.

This decision reflected something important I'd learned: When you discover something that genuinely improves your life, sharing it with others becomes a natural impulse. The conference wasn't just about business success; it was about holistic success that includes physical and mental wellbeing.

The Business Connection

The result of sorting out my health and wellbeing was what enabled me to achieve national-level success in my business. This wasn't coincidental. When you have more energy, better focus, and greater resilience, every aspect of your performance improves.

I found that I could work more efficiently, think more clearly, and handle stress more effectively. The irony was striking: by spending time on my health, I actually became more productive and successful in my work.

The transformation also gave me the physical and mental strength to take on challenges I never would have considered before. It gave me the confidence to attempt climbing the world's tallest free-standing mountain, standing at nearly 20,000 feet high, over 3.6 miles above sea level.

None of that would have been possible without Tristan and Owen. Their advice didn't just change my health; it changed my life.

The Mindset Shift

The message I want to share is simple: You don't have to wait until your health reaches a crisis point to make a change. I learned this lesson the hard way, but you don't have to.

I used to say, "I have to do a gym session." The language itself revealed my attitude: exercise was an obligation, a burden, something to be endured rather than embraced.

But I changed that phrase to: "My body deserves a gym session today."

It's a mindset shift, but one that turns an obligation into an act of self-respect. Think about it: Your body has been carrying you through life, supporting your dreams, enabling your achievements, working tirelessly even when you've neglected it. Your body has been there for you through late nights, stressful days, poor food choices, and countless demands you've placed upon it. After all that faithful service, doesn't it deserve to be treated with care and respect? Doesn't it deserve the gift of movement, strength, and vitality?

This isn't about vanity or achieving some perfect physique. It's about recognising that your body is deserving of the same care and attention you'd give to anything else valuable in your life.
Lessons from the Journey

This experience taught me several crucial lessons about health and wellbeing:

1 Health is an Investment, Not an Expense

Every pound spent on proper nutrition, professional guidance, and preventive care is an investment in your future. The cost of maintaining good health is always less than the cost of recovering from poor health.

2 Small Changes Compound

You don't need to transform everything overnight. Owen and Tristan helped me understand that sustainable change happens through small, consistent actions that build on each other over time.

3 Professional Support Makes a Difference

Trying to change your health habits alone is possible, but having professional guidance makes the journey more effective and sustainable. Owen and Tristan provided expertise, accountability, and encouragement that I couldn't have given myself.

4 Mental and Physical Health Are Connected

Improving my physical health had immediate positive effects on my mental state, and working on my mindset made it easier to maintain healthy physical habits. They're not separate areas; they're different aspects of the same foundation.

5 Success Without Health is Hollow

All the professional achievements in the world are meaningless if you're not healthy enough to enjoy them. True success includes being present and engaged for the moments that matter most.

The Ongoing Journey

More than a decade later, I continue to work with Tristan, and the principles Owen taught me remain central to my daily routine. Health isn't a destination you reach; it's a practice you maintain.

The habits I developed during those crucial years have become non-negotiable parts of my life. Not because I have to maintain them, but because I choose to. My body deserves that level of care and attention.

A Message for Those Still Waiting

If you're reading this and recognising yourself in the person I used to be (busy, stressed, putting health on the back burner whilst chasing other goals), I want you to know it's never too late to change your health status.

You don't have to wait until you're facing a crisis. You don't have to wait until you have more time, more money, or fewer responsibilities. You can start today, with small changes that honour the body that's been supporting your dreams.

The question isn't whether you can afford to invest in your health. The question is whether you can afford not to.
Your future self, your family, and yes, even your business will thank you for making that investment today.

Key Takeaways

* **Your health is your wealth:** No amount of financial success compensates for poor health.

* **Crisis isn't required for change:** You don't need to wait for a health emergency to prioritise wellbeing.

* **Professional support accelerates progress:** Working with qualified coaches and trainers makes transformation more effective.

* **Physical and mental health are interconnected:** Improving one naturally enhances the other.

* **Consistency trumps intensity:** Small, regular actions create lasting change better than sporadic extreme efforts.

* **Mindset matters:** Viewing health practices as self-respect rather than obligations changes everything.

* **Health enhances performance:** Better wellbeing directly improves business and personal success.

Actionable Steps

Today, identify one small change you can make to show your body more respect. This might be choosing water over another coffee, taking a 10-minute walk during lunch, preparing a nutritious meal instead of grabbing something quick, or simply going to bed 30 minutes earlier. Whatever you choose, frame it as something your body deserves rather than something you have to do. Notice how this shift in language affects your motivation and follow-through. Then, tomorrow, add one more small act of self-respect. Remember: you don't need a crisis to justify caring for yourself. Your body has been supporting your dreams; isn't it time you supported it in return?

What's Coming in Chapter 8: Reinventing Yourself at Any Stage of Life

In Chapter 8, we explore the power of reinvention and what it means to say yes to a completely new version of yourself.

I'll take you inside one of the hardest seasons of my life, when I was forced to question everything and start again.

This chapter will remind you that it's never too late to shift directions, rewrite your narrative, or make a bold new choice, even when it feels uncomfortable.

Whether you're facing a crossroads or simply craving more from life, you'll find hope, clarity, and encouragement to embrace change with courage.

CHAPTER EIGHT
REINVENTING YOURSELF AT ANY STAGE OF LIFE

"*You are never too old to set another goal or to dream a new dream.*" - C.S. Lewis

Have you ever looked at your life and wondered, "Is this it?" Many people do, quietly, often daily. But here's the truth: It's never too late to rewrite the next chapter. Whether you're 25 or 65, reinvention isn't just possible, it might be exactly what your life is calling for.

Reinvention doesn't always mean starting over from scratch. Sometimes, it means making space for something new to grow. A new direction. A new rhythm. A renewed sense of purpose.

The beauty of reinvention is that it can happen at any stage of life. Age isn't a barrier; it's simply a number that represents experience, wisdom, and the courage that comes from having lived through various seasons of life.

It's Never Too Late: The Recipe for Reinvention

Just next to our impressive, purpose-built building in Colindale sits a small, modest KFC. Most people walk past it without a second thought. But I often remind the team: Never underestimate what looks small. That little takeaway tells one of the most powerful stories of resilience and reinvention you'll ever hear.

Harland Sanders, better known as Colonel Sanders, wasn't a young entrepreneur or social-media personality. He was a man who faced more setbacks than most of us could imagine. His father died when he was just six. He left school in Year 7. Over the years he worked as a farmhand, tram conductor, railway worker, insurance salesman: you name it. He even trained in law, only to be struck off for fighting in court. By his mid-60s, he'd lost his restaurant after a new motorway diverted traffic away from his town, and he was left living off his pension.

But that's where the real story begins.

At an age when most people are slowing down, Harland was just getting started. With a pressure cooker, a white suit, and his secret recipe of 11 herbs and spices, he travelled the country, knocking on doors of cafés and restaurants, offering to cook his chicken on the spot. He was turned down over 1,000 times before someone finally said yes. That "yes" marked the beginning of what would become one of the most recognisable food brands in the world.

That's why I look at our building, then glance across at that little KFC with pride. Because it reminds me of what we're building here.

Colonel Sanders shared a recipe for chicken. We share a recipe for change. A way to help people cut the cost of their essential services. A simple method to create an extra income stream without giving up their day job. And just like Harland, we hear the no's. Dozens. Sometimes hundreds. But every yes changes a household and often, a life.

This building was made possible because of people who were willing to hear the no's. Sometimes thousands of them. That's our legacy. Just like Harland Sanders'.

So, if you're feeling stuck, worn out, or wondering if your time has passed, remember the man in the white suit. He didn't find his success at 20, 30, or even 50. He reinvented his life at 65.

Lesson from Harland Sanders: You can face a thousand rejections and still win. Reinvention isn't about youth. It's about belief and persistence.

It's Never Too Late to Change Direction: Neil and Sarah's Story

I want to share a special story that's close to my heart. It's a story of resilience, quiet courage, and the unexpected turns life sometimes takes, especially in our work lives.

Neil joined our business in 2003. What I didn't realise at the time was that I had actually met him nearly 20 years earlier. Back in 1983 or 1984, when I was a student new to Cardiff, Neil played piano at the church group I attended. Life has a funny way of reconnecting people.

Fast-forward to 2003: I'd sent out a few letters in the area, looking for people interested in joining my business. Neil was one of the people who responded. When we met, he opened up about what had brought him to that point.

Neil had worked for one of the UK's top banks. He was excellent with customers, deeply people-oriented, someone who genuinely cared about doing the right thing. But over time, the pressure to sell financial products he didn't believe in took its toll. Despite his objections, the pressure from his manager and the system didn't let up. Eventually, the stress led to a nervous breakdown, and Neil had to walk away from the career he had spent years building.

He was out of work for quite a while. But when my letter came through the door, Neil saw something different: an opportunity that aligned with his values and gave him a second chance to do meaningful work, on his own terms.

He started building the business part-time. It wasn't always easy. But over the years, he grew something remarkable. Neil and his team have introduced over 42,000 services, building a strong organisation that still continues to thrive today.

In August 2016, Neil sadly passed away from cancer. But the legacy he left behind is profound.

His wife, Sarah, had worked for the NHS as a practice nurse whilst raising their four children. Thanks to the residual income from Neil's business, Sarah was able to retire early. That income helped pay for their children's weddings and allowed Sarah to buy and settle into a new home. Today, she continues to run the business part-time, giving her the freedom to enjoy her grandchildren and support her family in new ways.

Neil will always be fondly remembered for his courage, his integrity, and the legacy he created.

Lesson from Neil and Sarah: When life forces you to stop, it's often an invitation to start something more aligned.

The Turning Point: Ian and Jen's Story

Ian and Jen joined our business back in 2007. Both of them were incredibly hard-working, but they were tied down in extremely stressful roles.

Ian ran a home-improvement company and poured everything into it. Jen managed a busy café with around 18 staff. Their working hours were long and relentless; they were like ships in the night. Ian would often finish at his own business, then head straight to the café to help Jen with stock and admin, sometimes working through to 1 AM.

The pressure took its toll. Ian actually collapsed from stress at one point. Jen was deeply concerned.

Not long after, they came across our opportunity. And what's incredible is that, over the last 18 years, they've built a residual income: a recurring monthly income equivalent to the returns of an £800,000 pension pot, all by helping people reduce their costs on essential services.

Ian was able to sell his business. Jen no longer works in the café. These days, they spend their time supporting their team and helping those less fortunate, especially through homeless charities they're passionate about.

They joined the business at ages 47 and 49. Now in their 60s, they're enjoying the benefits of that decision every day.

Lesson from Ian and Jen: Stress can destroy, but it can also wake you up to a different way of living.

New Season, New Story: Suzie and Sher's Journey

Sher was an Artist and later worked as an HR trainer with his wife Suzie, constantly travelling from city to city. Their "quality time" was often a quick dinner in a hotel restaurant if they happened to be working in the same place. Weekends were just about catching breath, repacking, and heading off again.

Then life threw them a few curveballs. Work slowed during the recession. Sher had a heart attack. Suzie's dad needed more care. They moved him closer and eventually, her mum too.

The opportunity to build a flexible income from home came at the perfect time. It meant they could say no to some of the long-distance jobs. Sher returned to his painting. Suzie spent more time publishing, gardening, and enjoying her parents' company. I remember calling and asking, "When was the last time you visited the National Portrait Gallery?" It had been a decade. So off we went. We met in London and had the most brilliant day. Same thing again in Cardiff at the Welsh Gallery. These are the moments that freedom buys you.

Suzie once admitted she thought they were too late. They were in their 50s and hesitated. But she didn't want to look back with regret. Sher was blown away by the diversity and warmth of the first training he came to. It was a room full of real people, from all walks of life, and that gave him the confidence to start. It was important to Suzie that they did it together.

Although she had some property, Suzie knew her pension wouldn't be enough, and she wanted to stay active post-retirement. Network marketing was the perfect fit: flexible, home-based, purpose-driven.

It wasn't easy at first. They had to learn new skills, step out of their comfort zone, and trust the process. But Suzie was determined. She believed in what was possible. And now? Their income is far beyond their first goal. They've paid off the mortgage. They've travelled to beautiful places. And the people they've met? Well, many of them are now lifelong friends.

Lesson from Suzie and Sher: What looks like "too late" is often the perfect time to begin.

The Power of Experience

What these stories demonstrate is something profound: Experience isn't a liability when it comes to reinvention; it's an asset. The wisdom gained from years of living, working, and overcoming challenges becomes the foundation for something new and often better.

Neil's experience in banking, despite the negative ending, gave him invaluable skills in dealing with people and understanding financial services. Ian and Jen's years of running businesses taught them discipline, customer service, and work ethic. Suzie and Sher's background in training meant they already possessed communication and teaching skills.

None of these people had to start from zero. They brought decades of experience, knowledge, and character to their new ventures. This is the advantage that comes with reinventing yourself later in life: you're not starting with a blank slate; you're building on a foundation of experience.

Breaking Through the Mental Barriers

The biggest obstacles to reinvention are often mental rather than practical. We tell ourselves stories about being too old, too set in our ways, or having missed our chance. But these stories are rarely based on reality.

Consider these common mental barriers:

"I'm too old to learn new things." Yet research shows that our brains remain capable of learning throughout our lives. Neil learned network-marketing principles in his 50s. Suzie and Sher mastered new technologies and business systems well into their 50s.

"I've invested too much in my current path." This is called the sunk-cost fallacy. Ian and Jen had invested years in their respective businesses, but staying on a path that was destroying their health would have been the real waste.

"It's too risky to change now." But what's the risk of not changing? Neil's breakdown forced change upon him. Ian's collapse from stress was a warning sign. Sometimes the biggest risk is staying where you are.

"People will think I'm having a midlife crisis." What others think matters far less than what you think. Your life is too important to live according to other people's opinions about what's appropriate for your age.

The Ripple Effect of Reinvention

What's beautiful about these reinvention stories is how they impact others. Sarah was able to retire early because of Neil's courage to start again. Ian and Jen now spend their time helping homeless charities. Suzie and Sher have created a network of friends and colleagues who've all benefited from their decision to begin something new.

Reinvention isn't selfish; it's often the most generous thing you can do. When you have the courage to change your life, you give others permission to change theirs.

Practical Steps for Reinvention

Reinvention doesn't require a dramatic overnight transformation. It can begin with small, deliberate steps:

1

Acknowledge Where You Are

Be honest about your current situation. What's working? What isn't? What would you change if you could?

2

Identify Your Assets

What skills, experiences, and knowledge do you already possess? How might these transfer to something new?

3

Explore Possibilities

Research options that align with your values and interests. Talk to people who've made similar changes.

4

Start Small

You don't need to quit your job tomorrow. Many successful reinventions begin as side projects or part-time ventures.

5

Embrace Learning

Approach new skills and knowledge with curiosity rather than fear. Remember, you've learned countless things throughout your life; you can learn new things now.

6

Embrace Learning

Surround yourself with people who encourage your growth rather than those who want you to stay the same.

The Perfect Time Myth

There's no perfect time to begin reinventing your life. There will always be reasons to wait: financial obligations, family responsibilities, economic uncertainty. But those same reasons will exist next year and the year after.

The perfect time is now, not because circumstances are ideal, but because you have the wisdom, experience, and courage to begin.

Are You Ready to Reinvent?

Signs you might be ready for reinvention:

- You feel stuck or unfulfilled
- You dread Mondays more than usual
- You admire others living with more freedom or joy
- You're facing burnout or a forced career change
- You find yourself saying "What if?" more often
- You feel like you're just going through the motions

If you ticked even one of these, reinvention might not just be possible; it might be necessary.

Remember, you don't need permission to reinvent your life. You don't need to wait for the perfect moment or the ideal circumstances. You just need to begin.

Colonel Sanders was 65 when he started KFC. Vera Wang was 40 when she entered fashion. Laura Ingalls Wilder was 65 when she published her first Little House book. Ray Kroc was 52 when he franchised McDonald's.

Your story of reinvention is waiting to be written. The question isn't whether you're too old or too late. The question is: what are you waiting for?

Key Takeaways

* **Age is an asset, not a liability:** Experience, wisdom, and skills accumulated over years become advantages in reinvention.

* **Rejection and setbacks are part of the journey:** Colonel Sanders faced over 1,000 rejections before his first yes.

* **Crisis can be an invitation:** When life forces you to stop, it often presents an opportunity to start something better.

* **Small beginnings can lead to significant outcomes:** You don't need to transform everything overnight.

* **Mental barriers are often bigger than practical ones:** Fear and limiting beliefs, not circumstances, are usually the real obstacles.

* **Perfect timing is a myth:** There's never a perfect time to begin; the best time is now.

* **Reinvention benefits others too:** Your courage to change gives others permission to do the same.

Actionable Steps

Write down one way you'd like to reinvent yourself in the next five years. This might be a new career, a new rhythm of work, a passion project, or simply creating more space for what matters most to you. Be specific about what this would look like and why it matters to you. Then identify one small step you could take this week to move towards that vision. Remember, reinvention doesn't require a complete life overhaul; it starts with a single step in a new direction. Your future self is waiting for you to begin.

What's Coming in Chapter 9: Finding Purpose Through Your Pain

Chapter 9 is all about turning pain into purpose.

I open up about personal loss, grief, and the internal struggles I carried through my teaching years, and how these experiences eventually became fuel for something greater.

We'll talk about how to process your own pain, honour your emotions, and use your story as a source of strength and connection.

This chapter is raw, real, and honest, and it's for anyone who's ever asked, "Why did that have to happen?" You'll leave with a deeper understanding of how even your lowest moments can prepare you for your highest calling.

CHAPTER NINE
FINDING PURPOSE THROUGH YOUR PAIN

I didn't grow up with a silver spoon, far from it. My childhood was full of challenges: emotionally, financially, and socially. Unfortunately, my mother's choices in partners reflected her own deep wounds and insecurities. My stepfather brought violence into our home, transforming what should have been a sanctuary into a battleground of unpredictability and fear. I developed the survival skills that many children in abusive homes master: the ability to read moods like weather patterns, to predict storms before they hit, to make myself invisible when tensions rose. The pressure on my mother was relentless. Eventually, that pressure became too much to bear.

I was nine when she attempted to take her own life.

The memory of that day remains visceral, the unexplained commotion, the whispered adult conversations, the arrival of strangers who would change our lives forever. We were taken into care, a clinical term that cannot possibly convey the emotional earthquake it represents to a child. I remember a social worker kneeling to explain what was happening, her words washing over me without meaning.

I recall the hastily packed bag, not knowing what to take or leave, what mattered or didn't. Most of all, I remember the sensation of my world dissolving beneath my feet, all certainty, however painful, replaced by a terrifying unknown. But over time, I realised those experiences were shaping something deep inside me: empathy.

It's strange how the very experiences that cause us the most pain often become the foundation for our greatest purpose. At the time, those difficult childhood moments felt like burdens I'd carry forever. The time my mother struggled bring up 5 children as a single parent I couldn't have imagined they would one day become the source of my deepest calling.

The Seeds of Understanding

Through sport, particularly running, I tapped into a secret source of joy. The release of those natural endorphins made me feel good. The success I found on the track and in cross-country gave me something to feel proud of. That sense of achievement planted a seed.

Running was more than exercise for me; it was escape. When life felt overwhelming, when the challenges at home seemed insurmountable, I could lace up my trainers and run. Every step took me further from my problems and closer to a version of myself I could respect. The rhythm of my feet hitting the ground became a meditation, a way of processing emotions I didn't yet have words for.

On the track, I wasn't the kid with the hand-me-down clothes or the complicated family situation. I was simply Derek, the runner. I was fast. I was determined. I was enough.

astles relay 10 miles = 53 mins

Originally, I thought I'd become a PE teacher. It seemed like a natural progression: take something that had given me joy and strength, and share it with others. But as I explored more of what education had to offer, I found myself drawn to the creative aspects of primary teaching: art, drama, music, and sport. I'm what you'd call a kinaesthetic learner. I learn by doing. I'm also a visual learner.

This discovery about my learning style was revelatory. For years, I'd struggled in traditional classroom settings, feeling somehow less capable than my peers. But when I understood that I needed to move, to create, to see concepts in action, education became accessible in a way it never had before.

Those early pains and the ways I worked through them eventually led me into teaching, not just as a profession, but as a vocation. It shaped how I led as a headteacher and gave me deep empathy for the children facing their own challenges.

The Weight of Shame

I'd like to share another aspect, a story that might throw some light on this journey from pain to purpose.

I always remember, as a youngster, my mother struggled to provide clothes for all of us. Many of them came from the Bring-and-Buy Sale at the local church hall. I was often embarrassed about what I had to wear. They were rarely new. And I always worried that someone, somewhere, might recognise their old shirt, sweatshirt, or jeans on me.

That sense of discomfort stayed with me for years.

Walking into school each morning was an exercise in hypervigilance. I'd scan the faces of my classmates, searching for any flicker of recognition, any hint they might have donated the jumper I was wearing or noticed the trousers that were slightly too short. The shame wasn't really about the clothes; it was about what they represented: difference, struggle, and not quite measuring up.

Children can be cruel, often without meaning to be. A casual comment about a "funny" shirt or "old" shoes could send me into days of self-consciousness. I learned to make myself small, to blend into the background, to avoid attention. Yet those experiences taught me something invaluable, what it feels like to be on the outside looking in. They showed me how shame can make a child feel invisible, lessons that shaped the empathy I later brought into my classrooms.

The Healing Power of Recognition

Years later, on a company trip to India, I had a completely different experience. One of my personal goals was to one day have a suit made for me on Savile Row, something perfectly tailored, just for me.

While in India, I visited a small fabric shop where clothes were custom-made. On a whim, I asked if they could make me a jacket and a shirt. The jacket, what's known as a Nehru jacket, with its distinctive mandarin collar and sleeveless design, was the first item of clothing ever made specifically for me.

It was a surprisingly emotional moment. To go from wearing hand-me-downs with quiet shame to standing in a shop having something made just for me: it was a milestone. It wasn't about the jacket. It was about healing, progress, and realising how far I'd come.

Standing in that small shop in India, watching the tailor take my measurements, I felt something shift inside me. This wasn't just about clothing; it was about worth. For the first time in my life, someone was creating something specifically for my body, my proportions, my preferences. The boy who had once worried about wearing someone else's cast-offs was now having something crafted just for him.

When I put on that finished jacket, I felt the full weight of the journey I'd travelled. The shame that had once defined so much of my self-image began to transform into something else: gratitude for the resilience those early experiences had built in me.

Finding Voice Through Vulnerability

Those early years taught me what it meant to feel invisible, to struggle with self-worth, and to question whether I had anything of real value to offer. But they also planted a burning desire to make others feel seen, heard, and encouraged. Without those experiences, I doubt I would have the same passion for people that I do today.

This realisation didn't come all at once. It was a gradual awakening, built through countless interactions with children who reminded me of my younger self. The quiet ones who hung back during group activities. The ones whose clothes weren't quite right, whose lunch money sometimes ran out, those unexplained bruises and expressions that seemed to carry the weight of adult concerns on their small shoulders.

In these children, I saw myself reflected back. And in seeing them, I began to understand that my own painful experiences hadn't been meaningless. They had been preparation: training in empathy, education in the tender places where people hurt.

When I stepped away from my teaching career, many assumed it was just a change of lifestyle. What they didn't see was the inner shift: how years of giving, leading, and holding it all together had taken its toll. I'd hit burnout. But in that brokenness, I found something more powerful: purpose.

The increased bureaucracy, paperwork, data, constant reports: it just wasn't my world. It was dragging me further and further down. The creative, relational aspects of education that had drawn me to teaching were being overshadowed by administrative demands that felt soul-crushing.

But even in that difficult transition, I was learning something important about the relationship between struggle and calling. Sometimes our greatest breakdowns become our most significant breakthroughs.

The Power of Truth-Telling

I started to share my story openly: first in small conversations, then in team meetings, eventually on stage. And every time I did, someone would come up to me and say, "That's exactly how I feel. Thank you for saying it out loud."

It hit me: the very experiences I once hid or felt ashamed of were the ones that helped others the most.

This discovery was transformative. For years, I had carefully curated the image I presented to the world, emphasising my successes and minimising my struggles. I thought that leadership meant having all the answers, projecting strength and confidence at all times.

But when I began to share the real story, the messy, complicated, human story, something magical happened. People connected not with my polished achievements but with my authentic struggles. They saw themselves in my challenges and found hope in my journey through them.

Sharing your "why" is powerful. It gives people permission to reflect on their own story, and sometimes rewrite it. There's something deeply healing about telling the truth: not the polished, picture-perfect version, but the raw, vulnerable truth. In our business, I've seen it time and time again: when someone shares their authentic story, their real reasons for seeking change, it resonates far more powerfully than any perfectly crafted sales presentation ever could.

The Ripple Effect of Authenticity

The transformation that began with sharing my story started to permeate every aspect of my life. In my network-marketing business, I found that people were drawn not to perfection but to authenticity. They wanted to follow someone who understood struggle, who had faced real challenges and found a way through.

This was particularly powerful when working with people from similar backgrounds to my own: those who had faced financial hardship, who felt overlooked by traditional systems, who carried the invisible wounds of not quite fitting in. My story gave them permission to believe that change was possible, that their current circumstances didn't define their future potential.

I began to understand that effective leadership isn't about being the strongest person in the room; it's about being the most honest. It's about showing others that struggle doesn't disqualify you from success: it qualifies you for compassion.

The children I had taught, the colleagues I had worked with, the team members I now led in business: they all benefited when I showed up as my complete self, struggles and strengths together.

Transforming Pain into Purpose

The journey from my difficult childhood to finding purpose through that pain wasn't linear. There were years when I tried to outrun my past, to prove that I had moved beyond those early struggles. I thought success meant leaving that version of myself behind completely.

But true transformation, I learnt, isn't about escaping your past; it's about integrating it. It's about taking the lessons that pain taught you and using them to serve others who are walking similar paths.

Every child I taught who struggled with confidence, every colleague who felt overwhelmed by the demands of their role, every team member who questioned their own worth: they all benefited from the empathy that my early struggles had developed in me.

The shame I had once felt about my background transformed into compassion for others facing similar challenges. The observation skills I had developed as that quiet child became invaluable in reading rooms, understanding unspoken needs, and connecting with people who felt unseen.

The Ongoing Journey

Finding purpose through pain isn't a destination; it's an ongoing journey. Even now, decades later, I continue to discover new ways that my early experiences inform and enhance my ability to serve others.

The boy who worried about his second-hand clothes became a man who helps others dress for success in all areas of their lives. The child who felt invisible became a leader who specialises in seeing and developing the potential in others. The young runner who found solace in movement became an adult who understands the importance of finding healthy outlets for life's pressures.

This doesn't mean that I'm grateful for the pain itself. Childhood struggles are real and shouldn't be romanticised. But I am grateful for what those experiences taught me about resilience, empathy, and the fundamental human need to be seen and valued.

Creating Safe Spaces for Others

One of the most significant ways my pain has transformed into purpose is through creating safe spaces for others to share their struggles and dreams. Whether in the classroom, the boardroom, or the living room, I've learnt the importance of fostering environments where people feel safe to be vulnerable. This means listening without judgement, asking questions that show genuine interest, and sharing appropriately from my own experience to show that struggle is universal and survivable. It means celebrating small victories and providing encouragement when progress feels slow.

In my business, this has translated into building a culture where people's "why" stories are honoured and where personal growth is valued as much as professional development. We understand that people's deepest motivations often spring from their most challenging experiences.

The Legacy of Transformation

As I reflect on this journey from pain to purpose, I'm struck by the realisation that our greatest struggles often contain the seeds of our most significant contributions. The very experiences that make us feel different, difficult, or damaged can become the source of our unique ability to serve others.

This perspective has changed how I view challenges, both in my own life and in the lives of others. Instead of seeing struggle as something to be ashamed of or quickly overcome, I've learnt to look for the gifts it might be bringing: increased empathy, deeper understanding, greater resilience, or a unique perspective on common human challenges.

The child in second-hand clothes taught the man in bespoke jackets about dignity and worth. The struggling student became the empathetic teacher. The overwhelmed headmaster became the authentic leader. And the irony is, that troubled 10 year student who was thrown out of school for being disruptive, is now helping to support that 10 year old orphan in Tanzania forge a better future. Each stage of the journey informed and enhanced the next.

* Our deepest struggles often become the foundation for our greatest purpose and calling.

* Childhood pain can develop empathy and understanding that becomes invaluable in serving others.

* Authenticity and vulnerability create deeper connections than polished perfection ever could.

* Sharing your real story gives others permission to reflect on and potentially rewrite their own.

* True transformation isn't about escaping your past but integrating its lessons into your purpose.

* The experiences that make us feel different can become the source of our unique contribution.

* Pain transformed into purpose creates a powerful platform for helping others.

Actionable Steps

1. **Reflect on your early challenges:** Write down three difficult experiences from your childhood or youth. For each one, identify one skill, quality, or understanding it developed in you.

2. **Identify your empathy triggers:** Notice which types of people or situations naturally draw your compassion. These often point to where your pain can become purpose.

3. **Practise authentic sharing:** Start small by sharing one genuine struggle or challenge with a trusted friend or colleague. Notice how this changes the depth of your connection.

4. **Look for serving opportunities:** Identify ways you could use your hard-won wisdom to help others facing similar challenges to those you've overcome.

5. **Create safe spaces:** In your current relationships and roles, practise creating environments where others feel safe to be vulnerable and authentic.

6. **Reframe your story:** Write your personal story focusing not just on what happened to you, but on what you learnt and how it equipped you to serve others.

7. **Connect pain to purpose:** Identify one specific way you could transform a past struggle into a platform for helping others, whether professionally or personally.

Remember: Your pain has prepared you for your purpose. The very experiences that once made you feel broken or different may be exactly what the world needs from you. Don't hide your struggles; transform them into your strength and let them become the foundation for serving others who are walking similar paths.

What's Coming in Chapter 10: The Power of Multiple Income Streams

Next, we take a practical turn and talk about money, specifically, how to build financial resilience through multiple income streams.

I'll walk you through the mindset shift that helped me stop relying on one salary and start thinking like an entrepreneur, even while working full-time.

You'll learn why diversifying your income is more than a luxury, it's a necessity in today's world.

Whether you're a teacher, leader, or professional in any industry, this chapter will help you reimagine what's possible for your finances and your future.

CHAPTER TEN
A PATHWAY TO FINANCIAL INDEPENDENCE

The pain you've experienced becomes your greatest teacher. That's what I discovered when my world came crashing down, when burnout forced me to re-evaluate everything I thought I knew about success and security.

Standing in that hospital corridor, facing the reality that my health was failing, I realised something profound: traditional employment, no matter how prestigious, had become a prison. I was trading my life for a salary, my family time for recognition, my wellbeing for a pension that might never come.

That moment of reckoning led me to explore something I'd previously dismissed: network marketing.

Now, if maths wasn't your favourite subject at school, bear with me, but I did my homework on these figures because I want to clear the air and debunk some long-standing myths about this industry.

For years, network marketing has been misunderstood, mislabelled, and even mocked. Yet behind all the noise, thousands across the UK and millions globally are quietly building financial stability, gaining time freedom, and creating a life on their own terms through this incredible business model. Let's set the record straight. What I'm about to share is based on real data, some sourced from Forbes, and backed by my own lived experience over the past twenty-plus years. This is a model that continues to change lives.

Myth #1: It's a pyramid scheme

This one needs retiring once and for all.

Pyramid schemes are illegal. Reputable network-marketing companies, like the one I work with, are fully regulated, and in our case, listed on the London Stock Exchange. We provide genuine products and services that help people save money and improve their lives.

The key distinction? A true network-marketing business rewards productivity, not just recruitment.

Think about it: every successful business has a pyramid structure. Your local supermarket has a managing director at the top, regional managers below, store managers, department managers, and shop-floor staff at the bottom. The difference is that in traditional employment, you can never earn more than your boss. In network marketing, you can.

Myth #2: Only people at the top make money

Not true. This industry is a meritocracy. You're rewarded based on effort and impact, not position or tenure. Some of the most successful people I know started after others but simply outworked them.

Compare that to traditional careers. Take education, for example: the Director of Education earns the most, followed by headteachers, deputy heads, teachers, and finally learning support assistants. No matter how hard an assistant works, they'll never out-earn the head.

But in network marketing? A learning support assistant can earn more than the director, because income here is tied to value, not titles.

It's one of the few professions where your results are driven by your actions, not your CV.

The numbers speak volumes:

- The global network-marketing industry was valued at £157 billion ($200 billion) in 2024
- Projected to reach £230 billion ($294 billion) by 2033
- Over 90 million people actively involved worldwide

Compare that to:

- Film industry: £23.5 billion (global box office)
- Music industry: £23.2 billion (global record sales)
- Video games industry: £150 billion (driven largely by mobile gaming)

Network marketing outpaces them all. This isn't just a side gig. It's a global economic force.

Myth #3: You have to be pushy or salesy

Absolutely not.

The most successful people in this space are listeners, not hard sellers. It's about service, not sales tactics. It's about understanding people's challenges, whether that's money, time, confidence, or freedom, and offering real solutions.

My teaching background actually gave me an advantage here. In the classroom, I learnt to identify each child's unique needs, to listen more than I spoke, and to guide rather than force. These same skills translate perfectly to network marketing.

Myth #4: It's not a real business

Tell that to the people who've paid off debts, left stressful jobs (myself included), or created generational wealth through it, like Neil and Sarah Johnson, whose story I mentioned previously.

In 2023 alone:

- Europe generated £20 billion in network-marketing sales
- The Americas: £49 billion
- Asia: £53 billion
- UK: £2.6 billion ($3.3 billion)

These aren't small numbers. This is a business done differently, but done well.

Why I chose this model over a conventional start-up

Determined to leave my stressful role in education I knew I needed an alternative. Starting a traditional business often means:

- High start-up costs
- Stock and storage
- Staff overheads

- Risk
- Long hours
- Delayed profits

And ironically, you become your own worst boss.

By contrast, network marketing offers:

- Low start-up costs (from as little as £10 to £100)
- No stock to carry or staff to pay
- Fulfilment handled by the company
- Scalable income with no fixed overheads
- Flexible working hours
- Built-in training, support, and mentorship
- Residual (royalty) income: getting paid for work you've already done
- A community of like-minded individuals cheering you on

In education, I rarely saw that kind of community. It was more about competition and comparison. This is different.

Myth #5: It's too good to be true

No, it's not perfect. But it is powerful.

Like any business, it requires commitment, consistency, and growth. But what many don't see is the personal development journey. You grow as your business grows.

As Randy Gage puts it in *The ABCs of MLM:* "*MLM* is a personal development programme with a compensation plan attached."

He's right. Your mindset, resilience, and leadership skills are sharpened. In fact, I used many of these principles in school, both with staff and pupils.

I get it. I was sceptical too

When I first encountered network marketing, my fixed mindset kicked in. "This can't be legitimate," I thought. "If it was that good, everyone would be doing it."

But that's exactly the point. Not everyone is willing to step outside their comfort zone, to challenge their limiting beliefs, to do the work required for real change.

My journey from classroom to climb taught me that the biggest barriers aren't external; they're internal. They're the stories we tell ourselves about what's possible, about what we deserve, about what we're capable of achieving.

Network marketing didn't just give me a way out of burnout and back into purpose. It gave me time with my family, a second chance at health, and the opportunity to help others do the same. It's not just about income. It's about impact.

That impact is like a ripple effect. One small stone thrown into a pond and the waves never stop. You can change lives. Starting with your own.

And by purchasing this book, you're already creating impact. You're helping a child in a small village near Moshi, at the base of Mount Kilimanjaro. A child who may be orphaned. A child in need of care, food, and hope. You're helping them climb to a better future too.

Road to the
Next Million
Road to the
Next Million

Key Takeaways

* Network marketing is a tool, not a guarantee. Success depends on effort, consistency, and personal growth. But for those willing to climb, it offers a pathway to both financial and personal freedom.

* Understanding that network marketing is a legitimate business model is only the beginning. Knowing the myths from the reality is one thing; actually succeeding in the industry is quite another.

Actionable Steps

Research and evaluate a business opportunity with an open mind. Look beyond the myths and examine the reality. What would financial freedom mean for your family?

In the next chapter, we'll dive into the practical side: how to actually build a successful network-marketing business. I'll share the strategies that work, the mistakes to avoid, and the mindset shifts that separate those who struggle from those who thrive.

You'll discover why your teaching skills, your life experience, and even your past struggles might be your greatest assets in this business. Because success in network marketing isn't about being the loudest person in the room or having the most connections. It's about being authentic, consistent, and genuinely caring about helping others improve their lives.

Whether you're considering this as a side income or a complete career change, Chapter 11 will give you the roadmap to approach network marketing with confidence and clarity.

What's Coming in Chapter 11: Making the Next Decade Count

In Chapter 11, we zoom out and look ahead: What do you want the next 10 years of your life to look like?

I'll share the reflective process that helped me gain clarity and set goals after years of uncertainty, pressure, and personal growth. This chapter will help you assess where you are now, dream about what's next, and make intentional decisions that align with your values and vision.

Whether you're entering a new season, recovering from burnout, or simply ready for more, this chapter will give you the tools to plan with purpose and boldness.

CHAPTER ELEVEN
MAKING THE NEXT DECADE COUNT

The next ten years won't look like the last. The world is changing, fast. With the rise of artificial intelligence, shifting economies, and global uncertainty, we can't afford to live on autopilot. If we want to thrive, not just survive, we need to be more intentional than ever about our choices.

Let's start with this idea: maintenance isn't growth.

Jamil Qureshi, the renowned sports psychologist, says it best: "Maintenance is not a good strategy." Why? Because when you aim to simply maintain, you're actually choosing to stand still whilst the world moves forward. Nature itself doesn't just maintain: it adapts. It evolves. It pushes back against resistance and finds new ways to flourish. And so must we.

Lessons from the Moving Trees

One of the most vivid reminders that nature is always on the move came during a trip to the Peruvian rainforest. We stayed at a remote lodge tucked deep in the jungle, a place where the sounds, the colours, and the sheer vitality of the forest were almost overwhelming.

There, amongst the tangled roots and towering canopies, I came across something extraordinary: trees that could move. Not in the dramatic sense of walking, of course, but these particular rainforest trees had root systems that looked like long stilts or legs, and they used them to slowly shift their position over time. If they were cast into shade, blocked from the sunlight they needed, they didn't give up. They moved. Inch by inch, over months or even years, they repositioned themselves in search of better light, a new chance to grow.

It was a powerful image. Nature can't control the weather, the storms, or the obstacles that fall in its path, but it adapts. It refuses to stay stuck. It finds a way forward.

Just like those trees, we too must be willing to move, to grow, to seek the light. Because Mother Nature never stands still. And neither should we.

This principle becomes even more critical when we consider the unprecedented changes happening around us. The past decade has brought disruptions that would have been unimaginable just twenty years ago: global pandemics, economic volatility, technological advances that are reshaping entire industries, and social changes that are redefining how we work, learn, and relate to one another.

The next decade promises to be even more transformative. Artificial intelligence isn't just changing individual jobs; it's reshaping entire economic sectors. Climate change isn't just an environmental issue; it's a business reality that's forcing companies to reimagine their operations. Remote work isn't just a temporary pandemic response; it's become a permanent shift in how we think about productivity and work-life balance. In this context, the idea of simply maintaining what we have becomes not just inadequate but potentially dangerous. Those who adapt and evolve will thrive. Those who resist change or try to preserve the status quo will find themselves increasingly left behind.

This is especially true when it comes to our health, our careers, our relationships, and our mindset. Whether you want to achieve something new or hold on to what you've already built, the real secret lies in continuous, consistent improvement.

1% Better Every Day

You don't need to make sweeping changes overnight. It's the 1% shifts that create momentum. Just like training for a marathon, you don't start with 26 miles: you start with a single mile, repeated consistently, building strength with every step.

The concept of marginal gains has been proven in elite sports, successful businesses, and personal development. When British Cycling adopted this philosophy under Dave Brailsford, they transformed from a mediocre cycling nation to dominating the Olympics and Tour de France. They didn't look for one massive improvement; they found hundreds of tiny improvements that, when combined, created extraordinary results.

The same principle applies to our personal lives. A 1% improvement might seem insignificant on any given day, but over time, these small gains compound dramatically. If you improve by just 1% each day for a year, you'll be 37 times better by the end of that year. Conversely, if you decline by 1% each day, you'll be nearly zero by year's end.

This isn't just mathematical theory; it's a practical approach to life change that I've seen work countless times. In my own journey, the transformation from being overweight and unhealthy to climbing Kilimanjaro didn't happen overnight. It happened through thousands of small, consistent choices: choosing the stairs instead of the lift, drinking water instead of sugary drinks, taking a walk instead of watching television.

I often use the GROW model, a powerful coaching framework that helps clarify and activate this process:

G is for **Goals:** What do you want to achieve? Be specific. Instead of "I want to be healthier," try "I want to lose ten kilos and run a 5K without stopping."

R is for **Reality:** Where are you now? What's working, what's not? This requires honest self-assessment without judgement. What are your current habits, resources, and constraints?

O is for **Options:** What choices do you have? This is where creativity comes in. There are usually far more options available than we initially recognise.

W is for **Will:** What will you commit to in the next 90 days? This is where the rubber meets the road. What specific actions will you take, and when will you take them?

This process doesn't just clarify direction. It activates progress, one meaningful, intentional step at a time.

The beauty of the GROW model is that it can be applied to any area of life: health, relationships, career, finances, or personal development. It provides a framework for moving from wishful thinking to concrete action.

The Power of Purpose

One of my favourite metaphors for purpose comes from nature: the salmon.

In Cardiff Bay, engineers built a barrage to close off the estuary and create a freshwater lake. This engineering marvel transformed the area, but it also blocked the ancient route salmon take to return upstream to spawn. Without intervention, this species, programmed to return to the exact spot it was born, would be lost.

So, a salmon ladder was created: a series of stepped pools, like watery staircases, allowing the salmon to leap their way back towards the rivers of their origin.

But here's what's so powerful: these salmon don't just swim upstream for fun. They face violent currents, crashing waterfalls, predators, and exhaustion. And still, they push forward. Driven by instinct, by design, and by purpose. Their journey is relentless, heroic, and deeply symbolic.

They remind me that there's a kind of beauty in struggle, especially when it's for something bigger than yourself.

This image of the salmon has stayed with me because it captures something essential about human nature. We all have an innate drive to return to our origins, to fulfil our purpose, to complete our journey. But like the salmon, we face obstacles, setbacks, and challenges that can seem overwhelming.

The difference between those who succeed and those who don't isn't the absence of obstacles; it's the presence of purpose. When you're clear about why you're making the journey, you can endure almost any how.

I think back to my own climb up Mount Kilimanjaro. That final ascent, beginning at midnight, was the toughest thing I've ever done. My lungs burnt from the lack of oxygen. My legs were heavy. My mind screamed at me to turn back.

But I kept moving. One step. Then another. And another.
There were no short cuts. No one could carry me. And yet, the summit came, slowly, steadily, with every step of grit.

The physical challenge was significant, but the mental challenge was even greater. At 19,000 feet, with oxygen levels at about half of what they are at sea level, every step required conscious effort. My body was telling me to stop, to turn back, to accept defeat.

But my purpose was stronger than my discomfort. I was climbing not just for myself but to raise money for research into motor neurone disease and also as a result if this book, for the profect in Malisita the school project we were funding, for the children who would benefit from the money we were raising, for the example I wanted to set for my own children about perseverance and commitment.

That purpose carried me through the darkest hours of the climb, when the physical demands seemed impossible and the mental challenges felt overwhelming. It reminded me that some things are worth suffering for, that temporary discomfort can lead to lasting fulfilment.

GRIT: The Hidden Ingredient

In a study of successful adults and children, researchers asked, "Who is successful here, and why?"

It wasn't IQ. It wasn't social intelligence, looks, or background.

It was grit.

Grit is passion and perseverance for long-term goals.

Grit is sticking with your future, day in, day out.

Grit is living life like it's a marathon, not a sprint.

This research, conducted by psychologist Angela Duckworth, fundamentally changed how we think about success. For decades, we've focused on talent, intelligence, and natural ability as the primary predictors of achievement. But Duckworth's work revealed that grit, the combination of passion and perseverance, is often more important than talent alone.

We've all seen it: people who quietly show up, again and again, in pursuit of something meaningful. They're not always loud. They're rarely flashy. But they are consistent.

I've witnessed this throughout my career in education and business. The most successful pupils weren't always the most naturally gifted; they were the ones who showed up consistently, who persevered through challenges, who maintained their effort even when progress seemed slow.

The same pattern held true in my network-marketing business. The people who achieved the greatest success weren't necessarily the most charismatic or the most naturally gifted salespeople.

They were the ones who made the calls when they didn't feel like it, who attended the training sessions even when they were tired, who continued learning and growing even when results were slow to come.

And consistency, for me, is the new currency.

In a world where everything seems to be accelerating, where instant gratification is expected, and where people often jump from opportunity to opportunity, consistency becomes a competitive advantage. It's the difference between being a shooting star and being a steady, reliable source of light.

The Consistency Chain

There's a great book called *The Consistency Chain* by Jim Packard and George Campbell. It speaks about how just staying consistent with even small actions can create compound results. The authors use the metaphor of a chain, where each day of consistent action adds another link. The power isn't in any single link but in the cumulative strength of the entire chain. Miss a day, and you break the chain. Miss several days, and you have to start building all over again.

If you've ever gone on a long bike ride, you'll know this: when you're climbing a steep hill, you can't stop pedalling. Even if you're barely moving, the moment you stop, you start rolling backwards, and faster than you climbed.

This principle applies to every area of life. In health, you can't store exercise for later use. In relationships, you can't bank kind words and gestures for future withdrawal. In business, you can't rely on past successes to carry you indefinitely.

So whether you're operating in mini, midi, or maxi mode, keep pedalling. Just don't break the chain.

And if you do fall off? Don't stay off for more than one day.

This is perhaps the most important principle for making the next decade count. We all have days when we don't feel like doing what we know we should do. We all face setbacks, disappointments, and failures. The key is to get back on track as quickly as possible.

I've learnt this lesson repeatedly in my own life. When I was building my health and fitness, there were days when I missed workouts, when I made poor food choices, when I let stress or fatigue derail my plans. The difference between long-term success and long-term failure wasn't the absence of these lapses; it was how quickly I got back on track.

The same principle applied to my business building. There were weeks when I didn't make the calls I should have made, when I avoided difficult conversations, when I let fear or complacency creep in. But I learnt to treat these lapses as temporary setbacks rather than permanent failures. I got back to work, rebuilt my momentum, and continued moving forward.

Purpose Meets Planning

We often think we've got all the time in the world. But time flies. And it can't be managed, only used more intentionally.

This realisation has become more acute as I've got older. In my twenties and thirties, a decade seemed like an eternity. There was always time to change course, to start over, to pursue new opportunities. But when I entered my fifties, I started to become more aware of time's finite nature.

This isn't meant to be depressing; it's meant to be motivating. When we truly understand that our time is limited, we become more intentional about how we use it. We stop wasting energy on things that don't matter and start focusing on what does.

Make the next decade count by:

- **Revisiting your purpose:** What matters most to you? What legacy do you want to leave? What impact do you want to have on the world?
- **Focusing on high-impact actions:** Not all activities are created equal. Some generate exponential returns, whilst others keep you busy without moving you forward.
- **Being consistent, even when you don't feel like it:** Motivation is temporary; systems are permanent. Build routines and habits that support your goals regardless of how you feel on any given day.
- **Surrounding yourself with mentors and growth-focused people:** You become like the people you spend time with. Choose your associations carefully.
- Adapting, evolving, and refusing to "just maintain": The world is changing rapidly. Those who adapt will thrive; those who resist change will struggle.

The Compound Effect of Decades

When we think about making the next decade count, it's important to understand the compound effect of sustained effort over time. The choices you make today don't just affect today; they compound over the years to create dramatically different outcomes.

Consider two people starting their careers at age 25. One saves £100 per month and invests it wisely, earning an average return of 7% annually. The other spends that money on immediate pleasures, planning to start saving "when they earn more." By age 65, the first person will have accumulated over £285,000, whilst the second will have nothing.

The same principle applies to health, relationships, skills, and personal development. Small, consistent actions compound over time to create remarkable results.

In my own life, the decision to start my network-marketing business in my thirties seemed relatively minor at the time. I was working part-time, making small amounts of money, learning new skills gradually. But over twenty years, that small beginning compounded into financial freedom, personal growth, and the opportunity to help thousands of others.

The decision to prioritise my health after my heart scare seemed like a response to crisis, but it became the foundation for climbing Kilimanjaro, maintaining energy and vitality, and modelling healthy behaviour for my children and hopefully, my future grandchildren.

The choice to share my story authentically, despite the vulnerability it required, started with small conversations and grew into speaking opportunities, this book, and the chance to impact people I've never met.

Reflection Exercise

Write a Letter to Your Future Self:
Think of the next ten years. Where do you want to be: physically, mentally, emotionally, and financially? What habits will help you get there? What excuses must you leave behind?

This exercise isn't just about goal-setting; it's about creating accountability to your future self. When you write this letter, you're making a commitment not just to abstract goals but to a specific person: the person you'll become.

Write a letter that includes:
Your vision for your life a decade from now: Be specific. What does your day look like? Where do you live? What do you do for work? How do you spend your time? What kind of relationships do you have?

The things you promise to start doing, and stop doing: What habits will you develop? What behaviours will you eliminate? What practices will you maintain consistently?

A reminder of your grit, your purpose, and your power: What will you draw on when things get difficult? What will motivate you when enthusiasm wanes? What strengths will you rely on? Seal it. Save it. Or better still, share it with a mentor or accountability partner.

The act of writing this letter forces you to think beyond immediate circumstances and consider long-term consequences. It helps you see the connection between today's choices and tomorrow's outcomes.

The Wisdom of Ancient Proverbs

"The best time to plant a tree was 20 years ago. The second-best time is today."

This Chinese proverb captures something essential about timing and regret. We all have moments when we wish we'd started something earlier, when we regret missed opportunities or delayed decisions. But dwelling on what we should have done 20 years ago doesn't change anything. What matters is what we do today.

The person who starts exercising at 50 might wish they'd started at 30, but they'll be grateful at 70 that they started at 50. The person who begins saving for retirement at 40 might regret not starting at 25, but they'll be thankful at 65 that they didn't wait until 50.

This principle applies to every area of life: learning new skills, building relationships, starting businesses, pursuing dreams, or changing habits. The best time might have been in the past, but the second-best time is always now.

Building Your Legacy

As we think about making the next decade count, it's worth considering what legacy we want to leave. Legacy isn't just about what we accumulate; it's about what we contribute. It's not just about what we achieve; it's about who we become and how we impact others.

Your legacy is being written every day through your choices, your actions, your relationships, and your contributions. The question isn't whether you'll leave a legacy; it's what kind of legacy you'll leave.

Will you be remembered as someone who played it safe or someone who took meaningful risks? Will you be known for your complaints or your contributions? Will people remember your excuses or your examples?

The next decade is an opportunity to be intentional about the legacy you're creating. It's a chance to align your daily actions with your deepest values, to make choices that will matter not just for you but for the people whose lives you touch.

What's Coming in Chapter 12: Reflections from the Climb

As we near the end of the journey, Chapter 12 offers a moment to pause and reflect.

I'll revisit the key moments that shaped my climb.

THE CLIMB

Arrival in Moshi

The heat hit me the moment I stepped out of the taxi in Moshi. The air was thick with dust and anticipation.

In the distance, through the haze, I could see it, Mount Kilimanjaro.

Nineteen thousand feet of mountain. Three and a half miles of purpose and possibility.

On the 28th of June 2024, I arrived at the Stella Maris Lodge, the starting point for one of the greatest challenges of my life.

Every challenge I've ever taken on has had a reason behind it. At first, this one was about health and fitness, a way to rebuild strength after the challenges of recent years. But it soon became something much bigger.

Purpose beyond the peak

A close friend of mine, who lives with bipolar disorder, once told me how he'd lost his father to motor neurone disease. His courage and honesty moved me deeply.

Around the same time, at one of our company leadership events, I heard an unforgettable talk by John Chart, who was also battling MND. His message, "Live for now, as tomorrow is never given", stayed with me.

So the climb became a fundraiser for MND research. And as fate would have it, the lodge where we were staying supported a local school for orphaned children right next door. That sealed it.

The challenge now had a double purpose: to raise money for research and to help the children of Stella Maris School.

"You don't climb just to reach the top. You climb because of what it represents."

I've always believed that purpose is the greatest motivator. Simon Sinek calls it 'starting with why'. It's what makes people follow a cause, not just a product. The same truth applies to life's climbs.

The journey begins

The expedition was organised by G Adventures, whose values instantly resonated with me:

1. Do the right thing
2. Love changing people's lives
3. Lead with service
4. Create happiness and community
5. Embrace the bizarre

And bizarre it was, setting off with a group of total strangers on a six-day climb to the roof of Africa.

We began at Machame Gate, hiking through dense rainforest alive with the chatter of monkeys and the calls of tropical birds. The air was thick and damp, the ground soft beneath our boots. As we climbed higher, the rainforest gave way to open moorland and the first sweeping views of the mountain.

By the third day, the path steepened toward the Lava Tower, a vast black outcrop from ancient eruptions. We camped beneath it, already feeling the thinness of the air.

Clement, one of the porters, became my rock, steady, patient, and quietly watchful.

The Wall of Fear

The next morning brought the Barranco Wall, a near-vertical stretch of rock that tested every nerve.

I've never been comfortable with heights, and there was a moment when I had to cross a narrow ledge with a dizzying drop beneath me.

My heart hammered.

"*Don't look down,*" I told myself.

One step, then another. Within seconds it was over and my relief was evident.

Preparation and Perspective

In the months before the climb, I trained hard, gym work, mountain walks, and mindset exercises. Some friends questioned whether it was wise given my health history, but once I commit to something, I'm all in.

"*There are no shortcuts to success. Everyone wants the elevator, but real progress means taking the stairs.*"

We live in an instant world, instant meals, instant money, instant results, but anything worth achieving takes patience, perseverance, and time.

That's where grit comes in. On Kilimanjaro, grit wasn't an abstract idea, it was real. It was each slow step against the thin air, each hour of exhaustion, and each quiet decision to keep moving when it would have been easier to stop.

It reminded me that in business, as in life, success belongs to those who keep going long after others give up.

The power of team

The porters were the heroes of the mountain. They carried our loads, sang to lift our spirits, and watched constantly for signs of altitude sickness.

Every morning they checked our oxygen levels, our heart rates, and how much water we'd drunk. Their kindness often came without words.

One evening, after a brutal day on rocky ground, I collapsed onto my hands and knees motionless halfway into my tent, too tired to untie my boots. A porter noticed, walked over, and quietly knelt to loosen the laces, slipping the boots off before walking away. No fanfare, no fuss. Just pure service.

Our group was a mix of characters: an Irish family of six, an Australian climber, a young man from Bridgend, and a Canadian beekeeper. By the end, we were bound by shared exhaustion and humour.

Everyone had their reasons for being there. Everyone had their own mountain to climb.

Summit night

The final push began at 10:30 p.m. on the 2nd of July.

The temperature had dropped to –22°C. The only light came from our headlamps, small dots snaking up into the blackness. After six hours of climbing, I was shattered. My water bottle had frozen, and my vision blurred.

I made the mistake of looking up, seeing the zigzag of lights stretching endlessly to the stars.

That's when the voice in my head began.

"*You're too old. You'll never make it. People die doing this.*"

Then I remembered something explorer Sir Ranulph Fiennes once said: "There will always be that voice trying to appear logical, finding reasons to stop. You have to fight it."

So I focused on the boots in front of me. One step at a time.

Slowly, painfully, the minutes passed until I heard a voice say, "*Congratulations. We're at Stella Point.*"

The relief was indescribable. The hardest section was over.

As the sun rose, painting the glaciers in gold and silver, I stood at Uhuru Peak at 6:24 a.m. on the 3rd of July 2024.

The view took my breath away.

Every ache, every doubt, every ounce of fear dissolved in that light. None of us reached it alone, it was a shared triumph of will and support.

The view beyond

Standing there, I realised the mountain was more than a climb, it was a metaphor for life.

Most people spend forty years climbing the wrong mountain, forty hours a week for forty years, only to retire on forty percent of what they earned.

We're taught to endure, not to live. To work ourselves sick for security we may never enjoy.

But change is possible. You can choose a different path, one of purpose, freedom, and balance.
"*If you want things to change, you have to change something.*"
Take one step. Then another.

That's how every mountain is climbed.

MOUNT KILIMANJARO
CONGRATULATIONS
YOU ARE NOW AT
HURU PEAK TANZANIA 5895M/19341FT AMSL
AFRICA'S HIGHEST POINT
WORLD'S HIGHEST FREE-STANDING MOUNTAIN
ONE OF WORLD'S LARGEST VOLCANOES
WORLD HERITAGE AND WONDER OF AFRICA

Key Takeaways

* **Maintenance isn't growth:** in a rapidly changing world, standing still means falling behind.
* **Nature teaches us to adapt and evolve:** like the rainforest trees, we must be willing to move towards the light.
* Small, consistent improvements compound over time to create extraordinary results.
* Purpose provides the strength to endure challenges and setbacks.
* Grit (passion and perseverance) is often more important than natural talent.
* Consistency is the new currency in a world of constant change and distraction.
* Time is finite and should be used intentionally rather than just managed.
* The compound effect of decades means today's choices dramatically impact tomorrow's outcomes.

Actionable Steps

1. **Identify your purpose:** Write down what matters most to you and what legacy you want to leave. Be specific about your "why."

2. **Apply the GROW model:** Choose one area of your life and work through Goals, Reality, Options, and Will to create an action plan.

3. **Start your 1% improvement:** Pick one small habit you can improve by 1% each day and commit to it for the next 90 days.

4. **Write to your future self:** Complete the reflection exercise, creating a detailed letter to yourself ten years from now.

5. **Build your consistency chain:** Choose one daily action that aligns with your long-term goals and commit to not breaking the chain.

6. **Eliminate maintenance mindset:** Identify areas where you've been just maintaining and commit to growth instead.

7. **Create accountability:** Share your goals and commitments with someone who will hold you accountable and support your growth.

Remember: The next ten years won't look like the last ten. The world is changing rapidly, and those who adapt, grow, and stay consistent will thrive. The best time to start was yesterday, but the second-best time is today. Make this decade count.

ABOUT THE AUTHOR

Derek Thomas is a former headteacher who made the leap into entrepreneurship, authorship and coaching, using his own story of burnout and reinvention to help others find purpose and freedom in their own lives.

After almost 30 years in education, including five as a primary school head, Derek stepped away from the profession he once loved when it began to take a toll on his health, family and sense of self.

Today, he runs a successful UK-based business that not only helps people cut everyday household costs but also supports them in starting businesses of their own. His first book, *From the Classroom to the Climb,* tells the honest and inspiring story of how he rebuilt his life from burnout to breakthrough. With heartfelt stories and real-world strategies, Derek offers guidance on resilience, mindset and financial independence.

Now, he coaches educators, leaders and individuals who feel stuck or stretched, helping them redefine success in a way that feels true to who they are.

Want to connect with Derek for further support or mentorship?

Go to www.derek-thomas.co.uk

Email: authorderekthomas@gmail.com

Printed in Dunstable, United Kingdom

71530600R00107